Conjure Codex IV

A Compendium of
INVOCATION
EVOCATION
&
CONJURATION

Conjure Codex: A Compendium of Invocation, Evocation & Conjuration
Content Editor: Jake Stratton-Kent
Art Editor: Dis Albion
Editor in Chief: Erzebet Barthold
Volume 1, Issue 4 : The Gold Issue
Copyright ©2020 Hadean Press
Cover Art © S. Aldarnay. 'Seal of Gold' redrawn from the *Clavis Inferni*.
All interior artwork © the original creators.
ISBN 978 1 907881 84 8
All Rights Reserved Worldwide.

No portion of this book may be reproduced by any means, physical or electronic or otherwise, without the written consent of the publisher.

"The Golden Guest" © Jack Grayle
"A Contemplation of GOLD " © Cath Thompson
"Shadowmancy and PGM's Rite of Helios" © Mani C. Price
"The Δαίμων and the Treasure" © Humberto Maggi
"Treasures of the Grave: A Practical Guide for the Aspiring Necromancer" © Gavin Fox
"Michael Scot: The Life of a True Magician" © Eldred Hieronymus Wormwood
"The Picatrix Decan Art Project" © J Swofford
"Aztec Solar Magic: Blood and Gold" © Erica Frevel
"Treasure of Heart Essence: The Revelations of the Great Yogini Sera Khandro" © Verónica Rivas
"Gold Ripens as much by Moonlight as Sun" © Victoria Musson
"Guns of Brixton" © Anthony Nine

Hadean Press
www.hadeanpress.com

This page intentionally left blank.

Conjure Codex

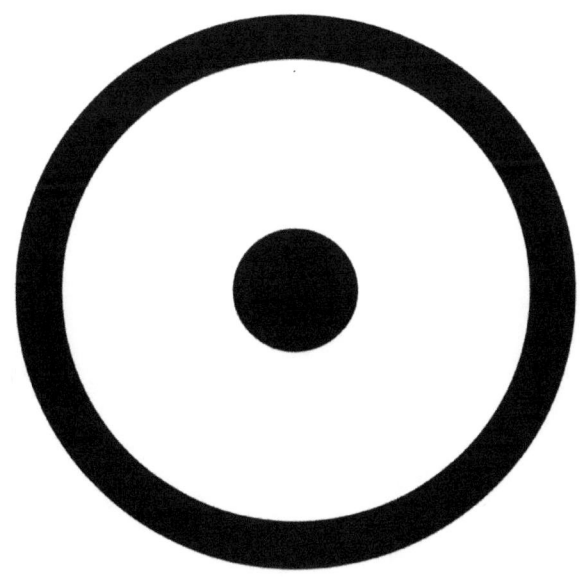

Edited by Jake Stratton-Kent
Dis Albion & Erzebet Barthold

Illustrations

Oxum, original artwork by S. Aldarnay — 4

Choleric Sun, original artwork by JM Hamade — 8

Marigold Petals, photograph by Jack Grayle — 13

The Son, original artwork by Mani C. Price — 23

Shabti Shrine for Hathor and RA/Khonsu, painted by Mani C. Price — 29

Brompton Cemetery, photograph by Erzebet Barthold — 47

Wizened, original artwork by Erzebet Barthold — 53

Picatrix Decans, original artwork by J Swofford — 65-68

Santa Muerte, original artwork by Erica Frevel — 70

Statue of Sera Khandro — 103

Singing Oat Field, photograph by Victoria Musson — 104

Mother Wheat, photograph and original artwork by Victoria Musson — 106

Grain Goddess 2019, original artwork by Victoria Musson — 109

The Sun, original artwork by Victoria Musson — 112

The Reaper of Grain and Life, original artwork by Victoria Musson — 113

Images from Space Weather Report, original artwork by Anthony Nine — 115-128

TABLE OF CONTENTS

9	Editorial Jake Stratton-Kent
10	The Golden Guest Jack Grayle
17	A Contemplation of GOLD Cath Thompson
20	Shadowmancy and PGM's Rite of Helios or as I like to call it: "Misadventures in Amateur Occultism" Mani C. Price
30	The Δαίμων and the Treasure Humberto Maggi
47	Treasures of the Grave: A Practical Guide for the Aspiring Necromancer Gavin Fox
54	Michael Scot: The Life of a True Magician Eldred Hieronymus Wormwood
64	The Picatrix Decan Art Project J Swofford
70	Aztec Solar Magic: Blood and Gold Erica Frevel
90	Treasure of Heart Essence: The Revelations of the Great Yogini Sera Khandro Verónica Rivas
104	Gold Ripens as much by Moonlight as Sun Victoria Musson
114	Guns of Brixton Anthony Nine
133	Reviews
136	Authors

WELCOME TO THE
CONJURE CODEX

Hadean Press excel themselves in this time of crisis with perhaps the most diverse volume so far of *Conjure Codex*. Herein we encounter an astonishing range of content. Magical plant lore, always a relevant and welcome topic, is represented by Jack Grayle's contribution, *The Golden Guest*; while Cath Thompson guides us in a *Contemplation of Gold* employing the English Qaballa. So too the Greek Magical Papyri are present and correct, in the form of *Shadowmancy and PGM's Rite of Helios*, from Mani C. Price. Humberto Maggi surveys the long history of *The Daimon and the Treasure* from ancient beginnings to the legacy of the grimoires and beyond. Matters necromantic – an important aspect of our magical traditions – are explored by Gavin Fox, and the important and strangely neglected figure of Michael Scot is ably handled by Eldred Hieronymous Wormwood. In our first *Picatrix* related contribution J Swofford explores the magical imagery of the decans in The *Picatrix Decan Art Project*. A fascinating and most welcome exploration of territory entirely unfamiliar to me is provided by Erica Frevel, in *Aztec Solar Magic: Blood and Gold,* So too we welcome Veronica Rivas' *Revelations of the Great Yogini Sera Khandro* dealing with aspects of Buddhist tantra. Victoria Musson brings us *Gold Ripens as much by Moonlight as Sun*, exploring the origins of poppets and their relevance to a broad range of cultures and their esoteric practices. Last but by no means least Anthony Nine delivers the *Guns of Brixton*, a thoroughly modern and culturally significant piece which pulls no punches.

Besides these stellar texts in the Gold issue, the reader will be delighted by the beauty of the pages, luxuriously embellished as they are. Thus, without more ado, I present *Conjure Codex* IV for your edification and delight!

Jake Stratton-Kent

The marigold that goes to
bed wi' the sunne;
And with him rises weeping.

Shakespeare
A Winter's Tale

The Golden Guest

Jack Grayle

When the prows of the Norman fleet first scraped the shores of Albion around 1000 AD, they brought with them rank upon rank of ruthless, well-organized and land-hungry warriors who excelled at fighting, taxing, writing laws and building castles. This tide of tyrants came attended by a secondary invasion of goats, geese, pigs, provisions, mead and men, children, sisters and wives (many who would soon be widowed). And amid the chaos of these unwelcome immigrants came many stowaways: some human, and some decidedly not.

One of the inhuman stowaways on the Norman fleet was most likely a scattering of Calendula Officinalis seeds. Only millimeters long, but shaped like Maori fishhooks, the small seeds would have clung to the ankles of dame and dog alike, and were soon scattered about the chalky shores of Essex, from whence they spread, thriving quickly until they (like their hosts) had conquered the better part of the British Isles. Unlike the Normans, however (who proved brutal and humorless overlords), the Calendula invasion was welcomed by the Britons, who found the plucky, bright flower both cheery and useful. Tough and hardy, it bloomed through every month of the year, but inspiring, when it converted grey fields to gold, peasants and priests alike noted how the flower opened at dawn, slowly swiveling its bloom throughout the day so that the gilded petals followed the sun upon its journey. On holy days, cunning-folk gathered its flower for its medicinal effects, which were many. Not only did it repel insects, but a distillation of the bloom's virtue was found to calm heart palpitations and mitigate menstrual ache, while a salve made from its essence soothed sunburn, healed skin lesions, and numbed nipples sore from nursing.

As a sign of their regard for the benevolent transplant, the Britons dubbed it Mary's Gold, or Marigold, after Mary, the Virgin Mother of Jesus, and a folk tradition arose around it to the effect that the Virgin had pinned to her breast the golden flower as a symbol of her love for the Father of her Son. Over time, as the Cult of Mary grew, so too did the flower's reputation, and eventually its advantages included the spiritual as well as the medicinal: a blossom kept in the left-hand pocket of one's trousers brought luck in love and law, and those who devoured the edible blooms might soon thereafter glimpse the Fair Folk. These traditions continue on in subtle strains of folk tradition to the current day, and the scientific benefits of the flower continue unabated as over 200 medical treatments now contain marigold extracts.

The following rite celebrates the marigold from the context of British cunning tradition. While it is my own invention, it incorporates techniques which were common in Marian medieval magic, such as the use of Psalms, gospel-quotes, angelic work, and the synthesis of Christianized myth with older classical legends, which were kept alive in part by the monasteries at the time. Indeed, this rite blends both "high" and "low" medieval magic, including as it does an extremely simple example of angelic compulsion in a much-distilled version of a goetic rite, along with some wortwork and rhyming such as could have been tossed off effortlessly by the eldest of beldames before the humblest of hearths. Its most eclectic ingredient is the reference to Marigold as the unlucky daughter of King Midas – an eighteenth century palimpsest attributable to Nathaniel Hawthorne's 'The Golden Touch,' which I hope the Reader tolerates, as it gives the lovely flower in question a tragic backstory, which no true beauty ever objected to. And as an American myself, I cannot resist leaving colonial fingerprints on British art/e. Thus, this rite is submitted in all humility, with the hope that it may bring the Reader (as the flower itself did the Britons of old) comfort, luck, insight, and joy.

MARY'S GOLD: A RITE TO FIND TREASURE

March 25th is the Holy Day of Annunciation – the day in the Roman Catholic tradition that celebrates the Archangel Gabriel's announcement to Mary that God had chosen her to bear His son. It is a day sacred to devotees of Mary, and highly appropriate for a Marian devotional and magical rite.

Therefore: On March 25th, pick three marigolds from a churchyard at noon, saying three Hail Mary's as you do.[1] Having done so, pluck nine petals from each flower, and tuck all twenty-seven into a Bible between the pages relaying the tale of the Annunciation (Luke 1: 26-38). Then put the three flowers in your left trouser pocket, and return home.

At dusk, take the petals from the Bible and arrange them on a sheet of white linen in the shape of the seal of Gabriel, as shown:

---

[1] The prayer, which was written concurrently with Calendula's arrival in Britain, goes as follows: "Hail Mary, full of grace, the Lord is with thee; Blessed art thou among women, and blessed is the fruit of thy womb, Jesus. Holy Mary, Mother of God, pray for us sinners, now and at the hour of our death, Amen."

Light three white candles, set them next to each flower. Say an Act of Contrition,[2] then ring a bell. Putting your hands on your chest, staring at the flower-seal, say of yourself:

BEHOLD YOU SPIRITS, ONE WHO WAS FASHIONED
BY HIM WHO SPOKE THE WORD AND IT WAS DONE,
AND TO WHOM ALL CREATURES ARE OBEDIENT; AND
BY THIS UNCHANGING NAME: JOD HAU VAU HAU
* AGLA * ON * TETRAGRAMMATON
I DO CALL YOU FORTH, O GABRIEL
TONGUE OF THE LIVING AND TRUE GOD
AND AS YOU ARE BEHOLDEN TO HELIOREN
LET MY VOICE BE YOUR TRUMPET
SO THAT WHAT I CALL WILL COME, AND WHAT
I BID TO BE WILL COME TO PASS. DO THIS,
LEST THE ALMIGHTY BE DISPLEASED,
LEST MARY BE DISTRAUGHT, LEST HER CHILD
WAKE WEEPING WITH HUNGER AND DISMAY.
QUICKLY, QUICKLY, NOW, WITHOUT DELAY!

Touch with the three fingers of your right hand the three flowers, saying:

MARIGOLD: O SUMMER'S BRIDE, WHOSE GAZE
MAKES DRUNK THE DREAMER; FLOWER
FAVORED BY THE MAID WHO BORE GOD
LIKE A FEVER: EVER TURNING TO BEHOLD HIM
AS HE ROLLED ACROSS THE ETHER; CALTHA
WAS YOUR NAME BEFORE HIS FLAME ERASED
YOUR PLEASURE. O MARIGOLD, INSTILL IN ME
YOUR HUNGER AND YOUR LEISURE. O MARIGOLD
REVEAL TO ME THE SOURCE OF MY TRUE TREASURE.

---

[2] "O my God, I am heartily sorry for having offended Thee, and I detest all my sins because of Thy just punishments, but most of all because they offend Thee, my God, Who art all-good and deserving of all my love. I firmly resolve, with the help of Thy grace, to sin no more and to avoid the near occasions of sin, Amen." This prayer, which is now an orthodox confessory, was developed by American bishop John Neumann in the late nineteenth century.

Take each flower in turn and pass it through one of the three candleflames, saying as you do:

KRYSOSTEPHEIS IO KRYSOPIS
PHAENNO PHAETHO BASILEIA

When you have finished, place the three flowers back into your left pocket. Then sweep the loose petals into the palm of your hand, and say, thrice:

I AM A SERVANT OF THE LORD: MAY IT BE
DONE TO ME AS YOU HAVE SAID.[3]

Put the petals in your mouth and swallow them. Once swallowed, put on the eye-glasses of one who has died within recent memory, but first, smear the two lenses with Chrism (consecrated olive oil). Having done so, walk outside into the late dusk.

As you walk outside into the semi-darkness, your vision blurred, proceed slowly and with care, taking time to taste the night air, to listen to those sounds you might otherwise have missed, to smell the tapestry of scent that underlies our world, mostly unnoticed. And let your consciousness attend those presences which have neither scent, nor shape, nor sound, but which may be detected by more subtle apprehension. Your blurred vision, and the marigolds in your pocket, may well result in a glimpse of fey or spirit for those who are sensitive to such presences to begin with.

Proceed to the highest hill or tallest tree that is in walking distance, then either climb the hill or tree as far as you safely can. Before dusk settles into night, at the crown of the hill or in the limbs of the tree, take out the first marigold blossom from your pocket. Holding it into your two hands, focus on its presence. Lift it up to your lips, and whisper to it these words, which reveal the flower's association with Marigold (also known as Zoe), the daughter of Midas, the Phrygian king who was granted by Dionysus the ability to turn into gold all that he touched.

MARIGOLD, CHILD OF MIDAS
AND HIS FAVORITE DAUGHTER
SEEING HOW YOUR FATHER SORROWED,
YOU EMBRACED HIM IN HIS ERROR,
AND SO ATTAINED TRANSCISSION WHICH
DID SILENCE ALL YOUR LAUGHTER;
FOR HIS GODSENT CONTAGION (NOT
DISCOVERED UNTIL AFTER)
TRANSFORMED BY CRUEL INFLATION
YOUR SUPPLE FLESH TO GOLD.

---

[3] Which is, of course, Mary's response to the Angel Gabriel's announcement that she will bear God's son.

Bury the marigold on top of the hill within the earth, or (if in a tree) between the bark and the trunk. Put your hand on the small grave, over the buried child, and say:

MARIGOLD, CHILD OF MIDAS
SLAIN IN BLOODLESS SLAUGHTER
GRANT TO ME A SUBSTITUTE
AND I WILL RAISE THE DAUGHTER
OF MIDAS WHO LIES BURIED HERE
MURDERED BY HER FATHER
AND REUNITE WHAT DEATH DIVIDES
AND TURN COLD TEARS TO LAUGHTER.
TELL ME OF TREASURE, AND I'LL RE-FORGE
YOUR FORM, TO FLESH, FROM GOLD.

Walk back to your home, again taking note of your surroundings and the attendant darkness. Once you arrive, take the second flower from your pocket, pluck the petals, and strew them in a line across the threshold to your door, so that no spirits may follow you inside.

Once you are safely within, pluck nine petals from the third and final flower and set them aside. Put the remaining petals of the third flower into a small pot with a cup of water and a fresh bay leaf. Boil the concoction, then strain it over a cup. Add honey. Hold it toward an image or statue of Mary, reciting The Magnificat.

MY SOUL MAGNIFIES THE LORD
AND MY SPIRIT REJOICES IN GOD MY SAVIOR;
BECAUSE HE HAS REGARDED THE LOWLINESS OF HIS HANDMAID;
FOR BEHOLD, HENCEFORTH ALL GENERATIONS SHALL CALL ME BLESSED;
BECAUSE HE WHO IS MIGHTY HAS DONE GREAT THINGS FOR ME
AND HOLY IS HIS NAME;
AND HIS MERCY IS FROM GENERATION TO GENERATION
ON THOSE WHO FEAR HIM.
HE HAS SHOWN MIGHT WITH HIS ARM,
HE HAS SCATTERED THE PROUD IN THE CONCEIT OF THEIR HEART,
HE HAS PUT DOWN THE MIGHTY FROM THEIR THRONES
AND HAS EXALTED THE LOWLY.
HE HAS FILLED THE HUNGRY WITH GOOD THINGS,
AND THE RICH HE HAS SENT AWAY EMPTY.
HE HAS GIVEN HELP TO ISRAEL
HIS SERVANT, MINDFUL OF HIS MERCY
EVEN AS HE SPOKE TO OUR FATHERS,
TO ABRAHAM AND TO HIS POSTERITY
FOREVER.

Drink the brew and go to bed, but not before taking the remaining nine petals and writing on each one one of the following letters:

G*A*B*R*I*E*L *X*P

Place them into a clean envelope or sachet, and whisper into it:

MARIGOLD, MARIGOLD, MARIGOLD
BY THE POWER OF THE ANGEL GABRIEL
APPEAR TO ME IN A DREAM, AT 3:33 AM
TO SHOW ME CLEARLY AND WITHOUT AMBIGUITY
WHERE MY TRUE TREASURE LIES.

Set your alarm for 3:33 AM. Upon waking, you will have seen your treasure: what it consists of, and where to find it.

The next morning, if you have indeed received a vision in the night according to the compulsion, return to the hill or tree and free the buried bloom of marigold. Return it to the churchyard, near where it was plucked, and thanking it, commend its spirit to the embrace of Mary, through the agency of Gabriel.

A Contemplation of GOLD

Cath Thompson

GOLD IS A MAGICAL WORD. Whether it's in print or spoken aloud, it conjures images of fabulous artefacts guarded by mythical creatures, or pirate hoards long buried, or of underground treasure chambers piled with coins and bars and trinkets of the shiny yellow metal. It's an oddly desirable substance; a bullion dealer once told me that in quantity it's almost hypnotic, it generates its own peculiar atmosphere of allure, and it's very beautiful.

By the simplest Doctrine of Signatures, gold has perhaps always been regarded as a Solar metal. In a society unbound by notions of personal wealth and commerce, the use and presence of gold would be a constant talismanic reminder of all things connected with the Sun, a material symbol of whatever spiritual qualities were assigned to the Solar power. (By "spiritual" I mean the contact area between mortal human and eternal universe, and the negotiations that go on there, in a very general sense.) The introduction of trade inevitably makes gold more valuable than most other commodities because the association of power is in itself the transference of power. However, it only becomes useful when it is traded for something else. You can't do much with gold, except enjoy the possession of it. It doesn't even need polishing. This is not a detraction from its spiritual qualities and association with the Sun. It's merely a reiteration of the natural Law of energy exchange, where gold simply represents the energy which must be spent in order to gain a particular result (ie, a different form of energy.).

So this little word "gold" has a whole lot of baggage behind it. We can arrive at a deeper understanding of its significance by investigating the word according to the English Qaballa. English words are open to Qaballistic analysis, not by translation into Hebrew or Greek but by the application of English Qaballistic enumeration to the English letters. (Yes, E.Q. is a "thing" and has been for nearly half a century!)

To begin with, the word GOLD has the E.Q. enumeration, G=11, + O=7, + L=2, + D=6 = 26. In this Qaballa the 26 letters of the alphabet are numbered 1 to 26. The value of GOLD is thus the same as the final letter of the E. Qaballistic alphabet. The number 26 is a maximal number, a quality beyond which one cannot reach within contextual limits. It's the top of its class, entirely appropriate as the numerical value of the name of a metal which is awarded for excellence.

The number 2 refers to duality, broadly speaking, and 6 is the value of LAW. To the E. Qaballist, the number 6 is a symbol of the concept of LAW, expressed by the harmonics in mathematics and geometry of the digit, parallelled by the characteristics of the 6th Sephirah. The distance between the angles of a hexagon marked on the circumference of a circle is the same as the distance between the circumference and the centre of the same circle, and that's just the way it is. (ARARITA!) So we can say that the duality (2) is part of the necessary structure (6) of the universe. To illustrate with another example of the number 26 symbolising Duality expressed as LAW: the word SHADOW also has the value 26, where the shadow of a thing is a feature of its illumination, and its doppelganger.

A further example is found in the word SON=26. The Son (anybody's son) is the reproduction of the Father (expressed as the Will of the Mother – but that's a different story!) – a chip off the old block as the saying goes. Similarities and opposites exist by necessity, and conflict by default. And that seems to be the way of things too.

To further explore the nature of 26 as a numeric symbol of Duality-LAW we will first look at the component letters of the word, their values and symbolism, and then attempt a comprehensible synthesis.

G=11. Both letter and number have been written about at length by various esoteric authorities, but there seems to be a general agreement that both are particularly mysterious. The number 11 is the Key to the order and value of the English magickal alphabet; it is also a reiteration in a united expression (the two 1's making one whole number) of the Duality of the number 2; its mystery is therefore dynamic and transformative.

GO=18. The dynamism is again expressed, as motion. The two digits are reminiscent of the wand and coiled serpents of the Caduceus. The values of G and O are 11 and 7; written together this is 117 which is the value of LETTERS, again suggesting the Herald and the bearing of a message. 117=GEMINI, the Sign of Communication. Here again we have the Duality of the Brothers, creative by destruction. 117 is also the value of THE LIGHT and is associated in E.Q. with the same characteristics as the 1st Sephirah in the Hebrew system.

If we combine the values of the last two letters L and D in the same way we get L=2 and D=6, 26, a repetition of the value of the whole word like a Qaballistic fractal, for extra emphasis.

GOL=20. Another indication of a dual condition, this time expressed in Zero as a potential (0=2).

So far, our E.Q. analysis has uncovered an aspect of gold which is actively communicative with no responsibility for the contents of the message. This is an unpleasant reminder of the trouble that the metal is capable of causing. It has an untrustworthy characteristic which corrupts and corrodes like a disease, an influence which is the dark flipside of the bright surface. It is the metal of the Sun, who also holds the barren desert sands in thrall, where he can kill a man quite easily.

GOLD=26 is shown to be a substance which is ideally suited to be set in motion, like a Son sent out from his Father's house to make his way in the world. It is only thus that the Father can gain any honour from his offspring, whose energy is that of a Key which by moving will release a lock and cause creative changes to occur. However, there is also a destructive impulse in its nature, which will manifest under conditions inclined towards inertia. Perhaps the ancients knew this when they said that gold was the excrement of the gods. Constipation can be fatal.

All of this confirms the correlation between gold and spirituality. Just as gold must be given for any material benefit to accrue, spirituality must be expressed for any alteration of consciousness to occur. To bring energy into manifestation, it is necessary to give energy, be it physically in the actions of a pentagram ritual or symbolically in gold coin. And here's the thing. Gold is heavy stuff. You can hoard it but you can't carry it with you out the back when the barbarians are at the front. It's too soft to make any tools with. Apart from in rare fields of electrical engineering, gold is only really any good for show, for trinkets, for decoration, and for Art.

SHADOWMANCY AND PGM'S RITE OF HELIOS

or as I like to call it:
"Misadventures in Amateur Occultism"

MANI C. PRICE

SHADOWS WALKING

I'M SURE YOU must have read stories like J.M. Barrie's *Peter Pan* or Hans Christian Anderson's *The Shadow* as a child. Do you know what they have in common? They both told of shadows that seemed to have a mind of their own. They left their owners at night to scout and do all sorts of amazing things, sometimes getting lost or ditching the original owner. Why would I bring up children's tales in reference to shadowmancy?

I was playing with my infant son when something dawned on me. I had noticed that he had been crying a few times while fearfully staring at the wall or certain points on the ceiling. I was trying to figure out what could be wrong when it hit me: my son was scared of his shadow! If you think about it, at one point or another we all were afraid of our own shadow. It is the darkness that always follows us. It mimics us, but often in strange or distorted ways. It can stretch, grow or shrink; changing its form as the mood takes it. This fear of our other, darker self has existed since the dawn of humanity. Even now the concept still holds a strong fascination.

The Ancient Egyptians believed that the soul of a person was composed of five elements or nine parts – it varied from dynasty to dynasty as the Old Kingdom entered into the New. To summarize though these components: the Ren (name), the Ba (the personality), the Ka (life force), the Sheut or Khaibit (shadow), the Khat (physical body), the Sahu (spiritual body), the Ab (intelligence), the Sekhem (form or power) and the Ib (heart).[1] The Ba (soul) was everything that made a person unique. It was the personality that passed on along with the Ka (life spark) into the afterlife. You know how certain people have out-of-body experiences? This is your Ba in the astral plane traveling while your body dreams.

The Ancient Egyptians believed the Ka (soul double) could only be sustained with food and drink. Although the dead could no longer consume the physical aspect, the Ka of the offerings could be.[2] The heart was believed to be the most vital since it was the key to the afterlife.

They believed the heart survived after death and gave testimony at the *Weighing of the Hearts Ceremony*.[3]

---

[1] Budge, E. A. Wallis (1967) *The Book of the Dead: The Papyrus of Ani* in the British Museum https://www.sacred-texts.com/egy/ebod/index.htm
[2] Budge, E. A. Wallis (1971). *Egyptian Magic*. p. 217-9
[3] Rhodes, Michael (2015). *Translation of the Book of Breathings*

Anubis (a death god) would examine the heart and place it on the scales. The heart would be weighed against the feather of Maat (truth). If heavier than the feather, it would be devoured by the monster Ammit (soul-eater). Your name (Ren) was believed to live as long as it is remembered. The ancient Egyptians, therefore, made it their business to put their ancestors' names on prayers and inscriptions with lists of their achievements. Names also had power and knowing the name of a thing gave you power over the thing. In cases of exorcism, the name was important to call, command and summon certain spirits.[4]

In the case of the Sheut, or a person's shadow, it is always present. It is impossible to exist without one and vice-versa. The ancients surmised that it, therefore, contained a bit of that person and contributed to their being. A person's shadow could be detached and captured. Shadow boxes with magical inscriptions were created for the Pharaohs to help protect their shadows from harm at night for just this purpose. A person's shadow could travel great distances very fast and had protective powers. It could haunt enemies; give them nightmares, cause insanity or worse. Statues of gods and humans were sometimes referred to as their shadows (i.e. shabti dolls) and employed as servants or protectors.[5]

In the *Book of the Dead*, spells #91, #92, and #188 were used to preserve the Sheut:

THE CHAPTER OF NOT LETTING THE SOUL OF A MAN BE HELD CAPTIVE IN KHERT- NETER.

"The Osiris Ani saith:- Hail, thou who art exalted! Hail, thou who art adored! Hail, Mighty One of Souls, thou divine Soul who inspires great dread, who dost set the fear of thyself in the gods, who are enthroned upon thy mighty seat. Make thou a path for the Spirit-soul and the Ba-soul of the Osiris Ani. I am equipped with [words of power]. I am a Spirit-soul equipped with [words of power]. I have made my way to the place where are Ra and Hathor.

    RUBRIC: If this Chapter be known by the deceased he shall be able to transform himself into a Spirit-soul who shall be equipped with [his soul and his shadow] in Khert-Neter, and he shall not be shut up inside any door in Amentet, when he is coming forth upon the Earth, or when he is going back into [Khert-Neter.]"

If a person managed to preserve all these elements, he would attain Akh status; a spirit with special magical abilities and allowed to live with the gods. Ancient Egyptians would write letters to the dead (specifically the enlightened ancestors who reached Akh status) for divine intervention in their lives. They would leave the letters at ancestral burial sites since they were considered direct spiritual portals to the underworld. These necromantic portals were accessible both ways. The dead could travel to the living and the living vice-versa.[6]

---

4 Budge, E. A. Wallis (1971). *Egyptian Magic*. p. 157
5 Rosemary Clark (2000). *The sacred Tradition in Ancient Egypt*. p. 292
6 Budge, E. A. Wallis (1971). *Egyptian Magic*. p. 219

Since the shadow is part of the soul of a person or thing, any magic that involved manipulating said shadows were considered unnatural and part of the necromantic arts. Since shadows were not bound to the grave, they could go anywhere. Shadows all belong to Anubis, though, and must return to the afterlife to serve him. Those that do not serve, wander the earth. This myth is probably the earliest explanation for shadow people and shadow men sightings.

Here is an excerpt from the Greek Magical Papyri (page 92) giving us instruction on how to awaken, summon and feed your shadowy servitor:

PGM III. 612–32

*[If you make] an offering of wheaten meal and ripe mulberries and unsoftened[123] (?) sesame and uncooked *thrion* and throw into this a beet, you will gain control of your own shadow[124] / so that it [will serve] you. Go at the sixth hour of the day, toward [the rising sun], to a deserted place, girt about with a [new] dark-colored palmfiber basket, and on your head a scarlet cord as a headband, behind your right ear / the feather of a falcon, behind your left that of an ibis.

Having reached the place,[125] [prostrate] yourself, stretch out your hands, and utter the following *formula*: "Cause now my shadow to serve me, because I know your sacred names [and] your signs and / your symbols, and [who you are at each hour], and what your name is."[126]

Having said this, [utter] the formula given above,[127] and in case he does not [hearken, say]:[128] "I have uttered your sacred names and [your signs] and your symbols, wherefore, O lord,[129] cause / my [shadow] to serve me." [And] at the seventh [hour] it will come to you before [your] face, and you address it [and say]: "Follow me everywhere!" But [look] to it, that it not leave you.

*Tr. J. M. Dillon. See the introductory note on *PGM* III. 494–611. This unique spell to acquire control over one's shadow may be part of the whole **Encounter with Helios** contained in III. 494–731. The Coptic section to follow (*PGM* III. 633–731) belongs with this section, and the mention of the "signs and symbols" in l. 625 connects this spell to the preceding; furthermore, the mention of the "formula given above" (l. 626) must refer to a formula given in the preceding spell, probably the formula found in III. 494ff. The appearance of one's shadow is thus the proof of Helios' appearance requested in *PGM* III. 494–731.

If one supposedly was to go to a field that isn't frequently trafficked at the sixth hour, counting from the start of sunrise, to make a specific offering to your shadow – would it really connect your shadow spirit self and bind it to do your will? It doesn't specify what astrological day/timing to perform the ritual, but I personally performed it on a Sunday (given the connection to the sun) at a solar hour.

THE RITE OF HELIOS

SHADOWMANCY IS ONE of the many aspects of necromancy as a whole. The Helios Rite in PGM, as you read, lists steps required to gain access to one's shadow in order to make a servitor. Last Summer Solstice, I decided to perform the rite as best I could to test this operation. I didn't know what to expect. Maybe a shadow person would show up (like the PGM mentions) after the rite is properly performed? I know I made a lot of mistakes but that's how we all learn. This is how I have learned why certain traditions or practices uphold through time and what things to discard through performance. Somehow there is a method to my madness.

I read and reread the relevant PGM chapters and verses. The rite was pretty straightforward. Go to a place that's deserted so no one will bother you. Face towards the rising sun. Bring with you an offering and carry everything in a new fiber-weave basket. It makes no mention of what to wear or how to dress. I am assuming anything white and made of cotton or linen is best. With a red cord, tie two feathers to either side of your head. One should be a falcon feather, and the other an ibis feather. I used a red scarf and hawk feather I found when I was in Arizona and a red ibis feather given to me as a gift (always adhere to your country's species protection laws and use common sense).

I looked like an idiot. I felt like one too. The offering I made was oatmeal with blackberries and black sesame seeds. Some ingredients were missing. I don't know what thrion is, and I had no time or money to go get beets. I did this totally on a whim. I don't know why but I felt compelled. It was like I was being told, "if you want to do this, you have to do this now or wait a whole new cycle." It mentions nothing in the PGM about what seasons or what part of the year to do this particular operation.

I took with me a beach blanket, a statue of Horus, my keys, my phone, a print-out of the PGM rite, the offering in a gourd, sage, a lighter, a wooden box, and a seashell to the park across the street from my apartment. It was secluded but hardly deserted. I live in the city. THE city. New York City. I would have to go somewhere upstate just to reach the deserted level PGM asks for. Everyone knows that's impossible as a fresh new mom. My husband agreed to watch our son for an hour or so while I was out doing this experiment.

So I left for the park, after giving a kiss to my baby and husband. Once at the park, I set up shop. According to PGM, it was to be done at the sixth hour of the day. I realized the night before it didn't mean 6 am like I had thought it meant. I was thinking like a modern person. First light or sunrise would be the first hour of the day, so noon or 1 pm would be more accurate. On a petrified tree stump, I placed my Horus statue. I rolled out the beach blanket, making sure I was under the sun. I gave sage to the area. I sat to meditate and clear my head. Then I followed the instructions from the PGM.

I read the Helios preliminary prayer. Halfway through I realized, "Oh damn! Half the prayer is missing! Not translated? Lost to history? How am I going to finish this?" I winged it by using names for Helios from the *Picatrix*, trying to remember as best I could. It still didn't help when it came to herbs, animals, trees, stones, etc. for each hour of the sun so I improvised from various sources (namely from memory). The iPhone was of no use. It had overheated and turned off! Did I mention this was supposed to be one of the hottest summers on record?

In my mind, at that point, this operation was a failure. People were around – not a lot but still enough. The prayer was incomplete. The barbarous names I was saying out loud probably sounded terrible and mispronounced. If I were a deity, I wouldn't answer me. I pushed through. I finished the prayer and then completed the second half making the offering.

Then I waited and meditated.

I waited some more.

It was hot…

It was really hot.

I was sweating.

I thought I was going to pass out.

I forgot to bring water.

I waited some more.

I prayed again and called out.

My stomach growled.

I thought I was going to pass out.

People were becoming curious. One person with a cell phone came up to see what I was doing pretending to be speaking to someone. That's when I decided to close up shop. Then all of a sudden for a brief moment, time stopped. The area around me became covered in a blanket of butterflies of all colors. Birds were coming out of nowhere all at once. I didn't know if it was a sign from Helios that he heard my prayer or it was all in my head and just nature doing its thing. So I left feeling stupid and ready to chalk it up as a failure and devise a new strategy to tackle this problem.

RESULTS

When I arrived at my apartment, baby and hubby greeted me with kisses. I put down all my stuff and took another shower to get the sweat off me. It felt great. My husband then proceeded to tell me that he heard on the news that this particular Summer Solstice was a record-breaking hot one. He was surprised I had been out there from 12:45 pm to 2:23 pm directly under the midday sun. At some point he left to go get groceries. I decided once the baby was asleep to start writing my findings down and chalk it up as a failed experiment.

Then this brain dump happened as I was typing:

Light cannot exist without darkness…

Darkness cannot exist without light…

So the Lord spoke

Praise unto Atum-Ra in the third heaven!

light … vision … voice … clarity … burning … piercing … hot… dry … serenity … peace…

Your shadow will cling to you until end of days,

All shall return to the land of shadows where their ancestors dwell

Point … zoom in … laser … focus and meditate

I am the voice that shot through all existence like a bang separating the waters

He who knows me shall have no fear

Ask of me what you will and it will be granted

I am the giver of life

I am the one who makes the barren women's wombs quicken with life

I am ray and the beacon

Come to me all you children!

I know all who I see and touch with my hands (light rays like fingers)

Shine ... radiate ... expand

I NN solemnly swear by this oath I make upon this hour to the lord most high to be the priest/priestess of light, the giver and keeper of the mysteries.

It is with this solemn oath I bequeath to you the knowledge and power over the spirits of light and dark. When you speak the word, when you speak the names, I shall come and obey. Now command thy spirit. Command thy shadow with a booming voice to obey and serve you.

Raise your right hand out. Look at it. Notice the light on the surface. Notice the shadow that clings to you. This is the true shadow. The other is false. A projection.

What does it mean to be a priest/priestess of the sun?

Power and understanding over nature.

Power and understanding over man's nature.

Exorcism of strange spirits from a place.

The vision of the sun. (Divinatory nature?)

Things that did not grow for you will now grow.

What the hell was that? I realized too late that at that moment the rite was not a spell or an operation. It was an initiation into the mysteries, and shadowmancy was just one of the things that could be performed by it. This was a rite of passage for someone entering the priesthood!

Oops...

CONCLUSION

I DON'T KNOW why it took another six hours for Helios to get back to me, or why there was such a long delay before receiving the transmission. I don't know if it was myself blocking it, people being around, or what. I do know that it takes light to travel 8 to 20 minutes from the sun to earth. This is the only explanation (and probably a poor one) that I can think of thus far.

I remember asking Helios why he responded, even after I got so many things wrong, like the names and so on. I got the feeling from him that what was important was that I had *tried*. I had put in the effort. I thought, "Surely I can't have been the only one to try this in the last few hundred years!" The reply was as immediate as it was oddly specific: "Only five, and three were translators." I was the sixth. I have no way of confirming this of course. Could there really have been so few people to make the attempt? I will never know. For all I know it's all in my head and I'm crazy.

I asked Laurie Romano her personal opinion on the matter, being an experienced Kemetic herself. I found her critique invaluable and it provided much food for thought. She suggested that the ritual's results might have been due to the nature of the spirit itself. One of Amun-Ra's epithets is "The Hidden One", or "One Who is Hidden", so it is possible this might have accounted for the delay in receiving the message.

My mother, a lifetime practitioner of the Luccumi faith, suggested the possibility that the entity in question was of course ancient and dormant. It took time to awake and respond due to its distance to mankind. Earth bound spirits who are continuously consulted will respond faster versus a celestial spirit rarely called upon.

Looking through my books on myths, history, occult, etc. I was searching for an answer – any idea really about what happened. I think I found a partial answer. There's an ancient Egyptian myth about Atum-Ra having a sister-wife consort named Iusaaset. She was the grandmother of the gods. Iusaaset is described as a goddess of darkness, his shadow, and right hand. She was described by the New Kingdom as the eye of Ra. Was Iusaaset perhaps the one I was able to reach? Did I accidentally become a priestess of Iusaaset? We may never know for sure, but it will be interesting to try and find out.

AFTERMATH

I AM FINDING myself creating more sculptural works than I did before, mostly consisting of spirits, deities or daemons. I have also found myself recently doing commissions for the creation of kemetic altars. Imagine my surprise upon researching Egyptian artifacts for one such altar and finding images that depicted the sun's rays with hands at the end, much like the vision described. There have been a few instance of figurine creation for clients asking for healing, domination and mental clarity. I can only surmise I am possibly doing the magical art spoken of by Helios. The modern shabti dolls seem to be quite effective thus far. I have not attempted any personal figures for protection or health benefits, though it should be interesting to see how those come out and record the findings. Regardless, this path has been fascinating to say the least!

I would love to hear your thoughts, comments, and feedback if any of you have attempted this rite from PGM. What response did you get? Was it similar or different in any way? I like opening a dialogue with fellow practicing magicians since this is how we learn – through trial and error.

The Δαίμων and the Treasure

Humberto Maggi

The verses of Homer are a treasure in themselves as the earliest surviving works of Western literature. Often in the *Iliad* and the *Odyssey* we find the first mentions of many subjects of interest to us magicians, like the first recorded use of the words δαίμων (daimon) and ἄγγελος (angelos) and the first description of necromancy. In them we also have the oldest record of a δαίμων giving and hiding a treasure.

The word *daimon* has deep roots that go far beyond the writing of the Homeric epics; its Indo-European linguistic origin links it to the idea of "distribution of riches". So, like Andrei Timotin clearly said, "étymologiquement, *le δαίμων serait donc un dieu distributeur (de richesses), faisant partie de la catégorie des dieux donneurs de richesses*" ("etymologically, the δαίμων would therefore be a god who distributes (wealth), belonging to the category of gods who give wealth").[1] This distribution of riches was mirrored in the function of the Indo-European king or leader who had the task of receiving and distributing riches amongst his people, his allies, and his guests. In the *Iliad*, for instance, we find Achilles, as the host of the funeral of Patroclus, distributing riches from his hoard as prizes for the athletic contests:

---

1 *La démonologie platonicienne: Histoire de la notion de daimon de Platon aux derniers néoplatoniciens*, Andrei Timotin.

But Achilles stayed the folk even where they were, and made them to sit in a wide gathering; and from his ships brought forth prizes; cauldrons and tripods and horses and mules and strong oxen and fair-girdled women and grey iron.[2]

The story of Achilles is a good place to start a discussion about the relationship between man and *daimon* and treasure. In fact, the whole *Iliad* revolves around the subject of distribution of riches: the wrath of Achilles that the poet sang of with inspiration of the goddess (the wrath that "sent forth to Hades many valiant souls of heroes, and made them themselves spoil for dogs and every bird"[3]) was caused when Agamemnon took Achilles' favorite slave from his share in the spoils of war. It when Achilles is drawing his sword to take his revenge that Athena comes to him:

While he pondered this in mind and heart, and was drawing from its sheath his great sword, Athene came from heaven. The white-armed goddess Hera had sent her forth, for in her heart she loved and cared for both men alike. She stood behind him, and seized the son of Peleus by his fair hair, appearing to him alone. No one of the others saw her. Achilles was seized with wonder, and turned around, and immediately recognized Pallas Athene. Terribly her eyes shone.[4]

---

2 Il. 23.226. In *The Iliad with an English Translation*, by A.T. Murray, Ph.D. in two volumes. Cambridge, MA., Harvard University Press; London, William Heinemann, Ltd. 1924.
3 Il. 1.1-4.
4 Hom. Il. 1.190-200.

The interesting thing that can be seen in these verses is the nature of the daimonic encounter described: Athena's epiphany happens in the midst of the assembly but only Achilles can see and hear what she says. In the Homeric verses the privilege of recognizing and interacting with a deity is reserved for a very few heroes, such as Achilles and Odysseus. Next, Athena advises Achilles to restrain his anger, and in harmony with the concept of the *daimon* as the distributor of riches, she promises him:

> For thus will I speak, and this thing shall truly be brought to pass. Hereafter three times as many glorious gifts shall be yours on account of this [Agamemnon's] arrogance. But refrain, and obey us." In answer to her spoke swift-footed Achilles: "It is necessary, goddess, to observe the words of you two, however angered a man be in his heart, for is it better so. Whoever obeys the gods, to him do they gladly give ear."[5]

Achilles's answer represents well the kind of piety we find in Greek religion, a religion where the interaction with the gods rests upon the idea of receiving favors and avoiding problems. The Homeric hero lacked posthumous hopes, and Achilles did not care much about the glorious gifts because his fate had already been foretold by his personal *daimon*, the goddess Thetis who was his mother: he was going to die at the walls of Troy.

The episode is relevant also because here we have the first register of the word "daimon": after talking to Achilles, the poem says that "she returned to Olympus to the palace

---

5 Hom. Il. 1.210-215.

of aegis-bearing Zeus, to join the company of the other gods."⁶ "Other gods" here translates to "δαίμονας ἄλλους".

It is in the *Odyssey* that the role of Athena as a riches-giving goddess is made very clear. After the many misadventures Odysseus suffered, during which he lost all the spoils of war and his companions, and was held for many years against his will as the lover of the nymph Calypso, he arrives shipwrecked at the island of the Phaeacians. The Phaeacians were influenced by Athena to give him gifts that surpassed the lost spoils and to take him home, and when she finally appeared to Odysseus in her true form she made that very clear:

> Yet thou didst not know Pallas Athena, daughter of Zeus, even me, who ever stands by thy side, and guard thee in all toils. Aye, and I made thee beloved by all the Phaeacians. And now am I come hither to weave a plan with thee, and to hide all the treasure, which the lordly Phaeacians gave thee by my counsel and will, when thou didst set out for home; and to tell thee all the measure of woe it is thy fate to fulfil in thy well-built house.⁷

I find this passage to be very rich when it comes to understanding the relationship between *daimon*, treasure, and fate. When he recognizes Athena, Odysseus first complains about her lack of assistance during the many years he wandered at the sea:

---

6 Hom. Il. 1.220.
7 Hom. Od. 13.295-305. In *The Odyssey with an English Translation*, by A.T. Murray, PH.D. in two volumes. Cambridge, MA., Harvard University Press; London, William Heinemann, Ltd. 1919.

But after we had sacked the lofty city of Priam, and had gone away in our ships, and a god had scattered the Achaeans, never since then have I seen thee, daughter of Zeus, nor marked thee coming on board my ship, that thou mightest ward off sorrow from me.[8]

Odysseus is being unfair in his ignorance; he is unaware that it was after Athena's plea that Zeus sent Hermes to deliver him from Calypso, that she acted upon the winds and broke the waves to save him from drowning, and that under the guise of a young maiden she guided, protected and advised him in the land of the Phaeacians, after influencing the king's daughter through dreams and putting a charm over Odysseus to help him gain her favor.

But the power of the *daimon* over her protégée's life is limited. Athena confesses that her actions were restrained because Odysseus had incurred the wrath of Poseidon; also, as her words above clearly state, there is a "measure of woe" that was his "fate to fulfil". Suffering, however, in the life of man, is not exclusively due to fate, as Zeus complains at the beginning of the *Odyssey*:

> Look you now, how ready mortals are to blame the gods. It is from us, they say, that evils come, but they even of themselves, through their own blind folly, have sorrows beyond that which is ordained.[9]

The δαίμονας often give advice that could avoid destruction but which goes unheeded. The advice given to Aegisthus, for instance, is mentioned in the very

---

8 Hom. Od. 13.287.
9 Hom. Od. 1.30-35.

beginning of the *Odyssey* as if foreshadowing what is going to happen to Odysseus and his crewmates. Many sorrows in Odysseus' voyages could have being avoided, if he and his companions had restrained themselves at a few critical moments; the "measure of woe" at his home was fated and could not be avoided. It was tied to the death of the suitors and the moment of death was a sacred fate that even Zeus did not dare to oppose (although it is hinted that he could have when he pondered saving his son Sarpedon at Troy).

Then we have the first narrative about a *daimon* hiding a treasure – the same treasure Athena gave to Odysseus she now helps him to hide:

> Be of good cheer, and let not these things distress thy heart. But let us now forthwith set thy goods in the innermost recess of the wondrous cave, where they may abide for thee in safety.[10]
>
> So saying, the goddess entered the shadowy cave and searched out its hiding-places. And Odysseus brought all the treasure thither, the gold and the stubborn bronze and the finely-wrought raiment, which the Phaeacians gave him. These things he carefully laid away, and Pallas Athena, daughter of Zeus, who bears the aegis, set a stone at the door.[11]

The *daimonic* treasure is now hidden and protected by supernatural means: the cave stone set by Athena could hardly be opened without the help of a god. Also, the cave she chose was not a common cave; it was "wondrous" because it was already enchanted.

---

10 Hom. Od. 13.360-365.
11 Hom. Od. 13.366-370.

The Cave of the Nymphs

The cave Athena chose was "the pleasant, shadowy cave, sacred to the nymphs that are called Naiads", where Odysseus before leaving to fight at Troy used to "offer to the nymphs many hecatombs that bring fulfillment".[12] When he recognized the place, he immediately greeted the nature deities:

> Ye Naiad Nymphs, daughters of Zeus, never did I think to behold you again, but now I hail you with loving prayers. Aye, and gifts too will I give, as aforetime, if the daughter of Zeus, she that drives the spoil, shall graciously grant me to live, and shall bring to manhood my dear son.[13]

The cult of nymphs was very popular and important in the rural areas of Greece. They were lesser divinities limited to a small geographical area, like a mountain, with a special focus on certain parts like a tree, a fountain or a cave. Caves in Greece abound and often have springs inside; that is one of the reasons why "the cave is the most common cult site of the nymphs".[14] They even had a few sanctuaries (a "nymphaion") where "oracular responses could be obtained"[15] inside sacred caves. A few chosen individuals could have access to "nympholepsy", poetic or prophetic inspiration by the nymphs that could happen, in certain cases, even by possession.

---

12 Hom. Od. 13.349
13 Hom. Od. 13.355-360.
14 *Greek Nymphs: Myth, Cult, Lore*, Jennifer Larson.
15 Ibid.

Amelasagoras (or Melesagoras) of Eleusis, the reputed author of a history of Attica, claimed to be wise (*sophos*) and prophetic (*mantikos*) because he was *ek numphôn katochos*, "overpowered by the nymphs."[16]

The *nympholept* (literally: "caught by nymphs") would be "someone who exhibited an unusual degree of religious devotion to the nymphs",[17] a person dedicated to the "maintenance of a specific cult of the nymphs, especially through the embellishment of cave sanctuaries".[18] Odysseus seems to be a *nympholept* of sorts as he used to give gifts and sacrifices to the nymphs at Ithaca. The caves where the nymphs had sanctuaries in Greece were in fact "treasure caves" due to the accumulation of votive offerings they received and, in the context of the *Odyssey*, Athena and Odysseus naturally expected their help in protecting the Phaeacians' treasure. Nymphs could be dangerous when protecting their favorite places, such as specific trees, and could kill people by drowning, for instance. They were also guilty of seducing and abducting mortals; the nymph Calypso held Odysseus captive for seven years. The association of the nymphs with death "became a popular conceit in funerary art and verse in the Hellenistic and Roman worlds".[19]

The Greek grammarian, historian and astronomer Asclepiades of Myrleia who lived for a time in Spain in the I-II centuries BCE recorded the legend that, during his adventures on the sea, Odysseus founded the city that

---

16 *Greek Nymphs: Myth, Cult, Lore*, Jennifer Larson.
17 Ibid.
18 Ibid.
19 Ibid.

would be later known as Lisbon in Portugal. The hard historical fact is that the region fell to the Roman Empire after a long and fierce struggle that lasted from 179 to 24 BCE. The Romanization of the peninsula, together with the Indo-European heritage[20] common to the Greek, the Roman and the Celtic populations of Iberia (reaching as far as the Upper Paleolithic[21]) helps explain the many similarities between the Nymphs and the "enchanted mouras" from Portugal. Like the nymphs, the *mouras* are local spirits associated with sources of water such as a well or a fountain, and with mountains and caves. The nymphs "haunt springs, caves, mountains, and groves of trees; they have the form of beautiful young women; they dance and weave":[22] so do the *mouras*. And the *mouras* are almost always associated with the distribution of riches: they "offer gold, treasure, or fruit".[23]

The Riches of the Dead

Hesiod introduces us to a different use of the word *daimon*. In his poem *Works and Days* he consciously avoids using the word to address the gods[24] and instead uses it to indicate

---

20 "The concept of nymphs as tree spirits is ancient. A belief in female tree spirits (and spring spirits) is common to many peoples speaking Indo-European languages." In *Greek Nymphs: Myth, Cult, Lore*, Jennifer Larson.
21 Portugal, *Mundo dos Mortos e das Mouras Encantadas I, II e III*, Fernanda Frazão e Gabriela Morais.
22 *Greek Nymphs: Myth, Cult, Lore*, Jennifer Larson.
23 Portugal, *Mundo dos Mortos e das Mouras Encantadas I, II e III*, Fernanda Frazão e Gabriela Morais.
24 With one notable exception, when the Ἑκατόγχειρες (hecatoikeires = hundred-handed one) Cottus addresses Zeus in a speech; he calls the supreme god "δαίμονι". But here the word is used not in the direct speech of the poet, but in a speech narrated by the poet.

the spirits of the dead men from the Golden Age; these spirits, however, keep the typical daimonic role of being "distributors of riches":

> But since the earth covered up this race, by the plans of great Zeus they are fine spirits [δαίμονές] upon the earth, guardians of mortal human beings: they watch over judgments and cruel deeds, clad in invisibility, walking everywhere upon the earth, *givers of wealth*; and this kingly honor they received.[25]

Hesiod himself under the daimonic inspiration of the Muses received a tripod in a poetic contest; tripods were valuable treasures for the Greeks. Important here is that Hesiod also expanded the use of the word daimon to include the dead; the dead could also distribute riches and the δαίμονές of the dead could later be invoked to become a magical assistant (*paredros*) who would be at the side of the magician to help in "whatever business"[26] he thought necessary or useful. The magical assistants were invoked to reproduce the original daimonic protection the magicians learned from reading the poems of Homer,[27] and that included, of course, the giving of riches.

The Homeric poems became a treasure map themselves. Following his passion for them Heinrich Schliemann would in the XIX century find the (incorrectly called) Priam's Treasure in the excavations of Troy and the

---

25 *Hesiod: Theogony, Works and Days, Testimonia*, edited and Translated by Glenn W. Most.
26 PGM IV.1928-2005.
27 Any person who could read and write in Greek was acquainted with Homer, as the Homeric poems were the basic school material to learn the language.

(also incorrectly called) Mask of Agamemnon in a burial shaft at the archaeological site of Mycenae. The Mask of Agamemnon was a funeral mask – a treasure of the dead. Another famous golden funeral mask was discovered on 28 October 1925: the Mask of Tutankhamun. The finding of Tutankhamun's funereal treasure became associated with legendary accounts of mysterious deaths; although untrue, these tales reflect the ancient idea that tombs and treasures were guarded by spirits.

Looking for the treasure of the dead was an activity as ancient as the burial of the dead with treasures: Tutankhamun's tomb "was robbed at least twice in antiquity" and "it seems clear that these robberies took place within several months at most of the initial burial".[28] After the Islamic invasion in the VII century, search for treasure in Egypt became increasingly popular. By the IX century there appeared the Arab *Book of the Science of Treasures* and guilds of treasure hunters were formed and even regulated by official laws. The different versions of the *Book of the Science of Treasures* apparently combined exorcisms and magical practices with lists of locations of tombs. According to the Egyptologist Peter Missler[29] it is here that we find the origins of the lists of treasure that became part of the Cyprianic literature in Portugal and Spain.

---

28 https://en.wikipedia.org/wiki/Tutankhamun#Tomb
29 *Las Hondas Raices del Ciprianillo*, Peter Missler.

The Treasure of the Devil

The earliest description we have of a pact with the Devil is found in the IV century Greek text *Confession of Saint Cyprian*. It narrates how Cyprian, after extensive studies, travels, and mystic-magical experiences, finally invokes the Devil and becomes his protégée. The association with the "father of daimons"[30] brought to Cyprian power, fortune and fame. After his repentance and conversion, he was granted extraordinary exorcist abilities.

These Cyprianic texts from the IV century are good research material for the process of "demonization" undertaken by Christianity against Pagan religions. The Christian *daimon* is now not just a fallen angel, but he hides under the guises of the Pagan gods themselves. The deities and the dead invoked in religious or magical ceremonies are considered to be fallen angels trying to deceive us. This process of "diabolization" was extensive and reached both the nymphs and the *mouras*. In Modern Greece the *neraïda*[31] "exists within a Christian matrix of beliefs":[32]

> Most informants in collected material on the *exôtika* indicate that the *neraïda*, like other *exôtika*, belongs to or is somehow allied with the devil. The *neraïda* is more often a cause of misfortune and disease or

---

30 As he is named in the anterior *Conversion of Saint Cyprian and Justine*.
31 "One often-cited example of the continuous survival of an ancient belief into modern times is the modern Greek neraïda. The term neraïda is derived from ancient nerêis (a daughter of Nereus, i.e., a nymph of the sea), though it refers in modern usage to a group of supernatural females who inhabit not only the sea but woods, springs, and wild places in general." In *Greek Nymphs: Myth, Cult, Lore*, Jennifer Larson.
32 *Greek Nymphs: Myth, Cult, Lore*, Jennifer Larson.

death than prosperity and health, while precisely the opposite was true for the nymph.[33]

In the same fashion, the Portuguese *moura*, even with her Prehistoric roots, was also enlisted into the infernal association, strengthening the idea that buried treasures are under the province of diabolical spirits. So, in one of the hundreds of ethnographic texts on these spirits we have:

> Still in Trás-os-Montes, in Onor River, Bragança, there is an enchanted moura at the bottom of a well, guarded by the Devil, as well as in Eivados, Mirandela, appears the moura accompanied by the Devil; in Sabrosa, in the castro known as "castle of the mouros" is said to exist a mine with strange beings, some say they are mouros, others the Devil himself. In Panóias, Vila Real, in Fountain of the Well, is an enchanted moura who lives with the Devil.[34]

The original Greek idea of the protective *daimon* that could help and give riches suffered then a metamorphosis that was also in harmony with the condemnation of wealth in general preached by a religion founded upon the denial of the world in favor of postmortem happiness. Not everybody was convinced, however. The old ideas survived in the hearts of people who were brave enough to consider that the devil, magic, and wealth are worth a try. And, contrary to the intentions of their creators, the Cyprianic legends helped foster this survival.

---

33 Ibid.
34 *Portugal, Mundo dos Mortos e das Mouras Encantadas I, II e III*, Fernanda Frazão e Gabriela Morais.

The Treasure of Saint Cyprian

The XIX century edition of the *Book of Saint Cyprian* that became very popular in Portuguese speaking countries is aptly entitled *Treasure of the Sorcerer*. The word *treasure* has here multivalent meanings. The book is, first of all, an extraordinary treasure of magical secrets whose roots can be traced to the magical *koine* of Mediterranean Antiquity. It offers ways to make a fortune-bringing pact with the Devil like Cyprian did, and also provides lists of treasures to be found. The association of magical books attributed to Saint Cyprian with the influence from the *Book of the Science of Treasures* brought with the Islamic occupation of the Iberian Peninsula gave rise to mixed treatises that could be used to locate and disenchant treasure. In lands so full of ancient memorials and legends, occupied in the past by Phoenicians, Greeks, Carthaginians, Celts, Romans, Visigoths, Vandals, Suevos, Alans and Saracens, the possibilities of finding hidden relics was too strong to be ignored. We can bear witness to the junction of the ancient ideas about the mouras and the *Book of Saint Cyprian* in the following excerpt:

> As we have heard, on the hill of St. Bartholomew are buried a large gold cask, which is guarded by a feral-moura or enchanted moura, an oil cask and a plague cask. The gold cask and the olive cask are of such value that they would make Portugal the richest country of the world if they were dug up, our informant told us, but the people do not dare to do it with fear of the feral-moura and the cask of plague, which is confused with the others by appearance. Several people have thought to disenchant these treasures, **using the Book of S.**

Cyprian. There were those who, one day, started the disenchantment. They traced in the floor, a sign of Solomon, pronounced the ritual words, but were afraid to continue, because then broke a furious cyclone; the trees began to crackle and earth to quiver.[35]

The *Treasure of the Sorcerer* also presents a delightful tale in which we can see present many of the themes discussed in this paper. It is the story of a French peasant named Victor Siderol who in a moment of despair accidentally invoked the Devil when he said to his tools "may the Devil take you". He sold his house and land and went to Paris in search of a better fate. It is there that he found "by accident" the *Book of Saint Cyprian* – when he was looking for a place to hide his own money. The book is then a hidden treasure in itself, and becomes the key for the peasant to find many other riches: "inside this surprising book, Siderol saw that he could put himself in close and magical relationship with the unclean spirit."[36]

The peasant then embarked on an odyssey of his own; he studied the book and performed successfully the ritual of invocation. After that, the Devil became his guide and patron, taking him through many adventures until he found his treasure and a good marriage. The Devil surprisingly and constantly gives the peasant pious and good advice, that he often ignores to his own loss. Like Athena with Odysseus, the Devil also at times created trials for his protégée, and like the deities of ancient times he did not take lightly Victor's faults:

---

[35] *Portugal, Mundo dos Mortos e das Mouras Encantadas I, II e III*, Fernanda Frazão e Gabriela Morais.
[36] *The Book of Saint Cyprian*, Humberto Maggi.

Did I not tell you already, false friend, that my law requires patience? I did not give you food to eat to try your courage. Go, then, to your destiny, and do not betray me again, or else…[37]

The treasure disenchanted by the peasant was a "large lattice containing golden Roman coins"; speaking for the perennial fascination old treasure still holds, we all heard about the "soapstone amphora" found "at the bottom of the Cressoni Theatre in Como, northern Italy", in September 2018:

> Inside was an estimated 300 gold coins from the late Roman Imperial era, which took place in the 5th century, just before the empire's untimely demise. Despite their age, the coins are in miraculous condition, with all the images and engravings easily visible. [38]

We often hear of finds like that, but in none of these modern findings is there a mention of magic. Old treasure is found generally by the meticulous search of archaeologists; that is how we recuperated the fortunes romantically assigned to Priam and Agamemnon. Now and then fortune smiles upon average people who encounter treasure by accident, and amateur metal detectorists can be lucky even when looking for something else: the largest cache of Roman gold was found in Britain by a retired gardener helping a friend who lost a hammer. Ancient Greeks would see in these incidents the mysterious intervention of daimonic

---

37 Ibid.
38 https://www.sciencealert.com/a-pot-of-5th-century-gold-coins-have-been-found-under-an-italian-theatre

forces in the lives of a few chosen. *Daimon* and fate were considered to be forces often in conflict, but even Zeus in the end submitted to the fate determined for his son Sarpedon. To what extent can the magician enlist daimonic help? To what extent does the daimon wish to intervene?

Treasures of the Grave
A Practical Guide for the Aspiring Necromancer

Gavin Fox

As a modern necromancer my personal path is one centred around respectfully working with the actual energies of the dead, the memetic concept of death as a social construct, and the inherent life force in all things as well. This multi-faceted approach owes much to the wider discipline of chaos magick, and allows a great deal of flexibility for me to do as I wilt in developing a viable methodology all of my own. Considering that I have nothing but the greatest respect for those who have journeyed to the lands beyond the veil, my continued exploration of the entropic arts is steered by a well defined moral code. I would never wish to popularise or condone the practice of digging up human remains, nor do I find any value in stealing artefacts from inside the grave itself. Not only would such trinkets be next to useless to any necromant wishing to follow in my footsteps, but there are easier treasures out there just waiting to be harvested anyway.

Growing up in London I was lucky enough to have access to a number of shops that were dedicated to providing supplies for the wider occult community. But as any urban magickian will tell you, all those pre-packaged inks, powders and candles can only go so far. As soon as you deviate from the usual circle and sage methodology you are bound to find it hard to find what you are looking for, even online. Especially if, like me, you are more interested in the dead than the living. And yet necromantic supplies are freely available within a few miles of your home, if you have the tenacity to go find them. Every city has its graveyards, and every square foot of their overgrown and neglected floor plan is a treasure-trove of ingredients for the seeker and adept alike.

If you have any real interest in connecting with either the death current or the unquiet dead in general, you will need to acquire some grave dirt. A mainstay of the necromantic paradigm, this soil allows you to bring a piece of the cemetery home with you and helps create a connection to the underworld within an otherwise mundane space. It can also be used in any general working dealing with the discarnate, and a small freshly harvested bowl left in your magickal laboratory or on a more traditional ancestor altar will keep it tuned for months with little extra maintenance needed. That said, it works best as an ingredient in more complex blends, and the extra time spent hunched over the mixing bowl tends to be worthwhile in the long run.

Foxfire Powder

The first magickal recipe I have decided to share is something of a workhorse. At its core lies an amalgamation of innocent ingredients freely available in pretty much any town with both a supermarket and a graveyard, but it soon becomes potent beyond measure when combined in the manner I describe. Infinitely adaptable and easily stored for months at a time, foxfire powder is my first choice for hands-on banishing, cleansing and purification, though it smells beyond terrible and will stain if mixed with either oil or water. The liquid version also kills plants and repels animals who rely on scent to navigate the world around them, though this aspect is generally of limited use to the necromant unless they have a long running feud with next door's dog.

The most basic foxfire blend involves mixing equal parts grave soil, good quality sea salt, unmagnetised iron filings, dried garlic powder and powdered chalk in a large resealable glass jar, before placing it under the earth for a full lunar month. This step is designed to be symbolic of burial, and as such a short funerary service involving the underworld godforms of the necromancer's choice should be intoned as the container is lowered into the ground. Thankfully, this process does not need to be undertaken in a cemetery to be to be effective, and as such the magickian should be able to avoid the risk of getting caught by less enlightened individuals while working on a fresh batch.

The necromancer can further elaborate upon the blend by adding secondary ingredients such as coffin nails, grave glass, frankincense resin and silver sixpences; spring water and extra virgin olive oil should the liquid version be preferred. The mixture can then be carried in pouches and bottles for protection or poured through funnels to draw circles and sigils as needed. Foxfire is a pretty forgiving material to work with, aside from the smell, and it should retain its effectiveness even if time constraints negate the possibility of allowing the powder to properly age in the womb of the Earth before use.

While there are a few professional brands of grave soil on the market, as with anything mass produced and sold for a premium it is better to find your own. This is by far one of the hardest items to get a hold of without getting caught, however, but a small sandwich bag-full is easy enough to smuggle past the graveyard attendants if you are discreet and confident in what you are doing.

Pre-planning comes into play here, as it is essential to know where to dig without being seen. Understanding the history of the grave you are harvesting from is useful as well, though this preliminary research can be skipped should supplies run low and a familiar burial site becomes unavailable. That oversight will have a direct effect on the potency of the powder or outcome of the ritual that you undertake, however, as every internment has a flavour all of its own.

Soldiers and police will work best for protection blends, for example, while murderers and criminals are especially tailored for hexing. For the least squeamish, the graves of friends and family can be sought out and thus their occupants invited back into your home for a variety of reasons. Fresh burials may be easier to harvest, but older ones have soaked up more energy, ageing like a fine wine until they hum under the magickian's fingers and signal their readiness. While the ground is usually a little harder to break, the pay-off tends to be worth it in the long run. A few inches should be deep enough to get what you need, and the drier the better; you're harvesting grave soil, not swamp mud after all.

Taking some dirt can leave a neat little space to place something else that needs charging by the death current for retrieval at a later date, such as an amulet, crystal or figurine. These are best left for a lunar month, new moon to new moon, and will hold said charge for another month or so once removed from the grave. It is worth taking into account the very real possibility of another necromant digging it up by accident while harvesting their own grave soil, however, so the less valuable the better is a good rule of thumb here.

Next we come to a personal favourite of mine, grave glass. Not those annoying little candles you see kicked to pieces all over the place when you go to walk among the dead, but the multicoloured chips that cover the tops of graves in more modern cemeteries. While glass in general is not crystalline and has therefore been traditionally overlooked by magickians and pagans alike, it can still be put to use in a ritualistic context. Regardless of colour this particular tool behaves much like one of the buried items mentioned earlier, and is best harvested around the time of the new moon. Due to the long term saturation by the death current, in certain cases in excess of twenty or thirty years, it will retain its charge almost indefinitely and very rarely needs replacing unless drained deliberately.

Grave Glass Cookies

Whether you choose to create either the classic repelling grave glass cookies or the more necromantically minded attracting version, the construction methodology is pretty much the same. First take enough air drying terracotta modelling clay as is needed, denoted by the individual size and overall amount of cookies that you desire, and slice it into roughly equal portions. Roll these between your hands until they are round, and then gently flatten them against the greaseproof paper with your palm. Ideally, you will need to leave the clay at least an inch thick, perhaps a little more raised in the centre, so that it can receive the items that you will be pressing into its surface.

For the repelling cookies, first press either a bloodstone or obsidian chunk into the middle of each flattened piece of clay. Then working outward, add five iron nails; pressing them upward through the underside of the cookie or downward through the top depending upon your preference for sharp or blunt tips. Finally, apply the shards of grave glass in a similar fashion, forming the final ring on the very outermost edges of the clay disk. These should face upward in line with the position of the nails and again either sharp or blunt depending upon the style chosen for the previous step. The attracting cookies are made in exactly the same way, but this time the central stone should either consist of smoky quartz or amethyst, the iron nails being replaced with fragments of animal bone in an effort to invite memories of physicality in the unseen interloper and hopefully entice it to stay. Once the modelling material has hardened, place the cookies facing the doors and windows of your home and await the results.

Grave glass has a number of uses aside from creating cookies. In hexing operations it can be pressed through a clay effigy or photograph of an enemy, stimulating the release of concentrated death energy within their body at the locations punctured through sympathetic magick. And of course, it can also just be left in the necromancer's laboratory to add its unique resonance to that of your other magickal trinkets and tools too. It does not grind well, however, and unlike the more versatile grave soil must be used whole for the best effect. Whether that limits its usefulness really depends upon your imagination, and ingenuity when putting such rituals together for the first time.

If you do not wish to disturb those that were once human, or do not follow a path that has much to do with them, cemeteries still hold a host of useful treasures. Feathers are usually easy to find, as are animal bones, especially if there is a skulk of foxes or groups of other predatory animals living in the area. For me at least, such items are always a nice surprise when walking those winding, ivy shadowed pathways for other reasons, and it is recommended that a small cloth bag be taken on such day trips just in case the opportunity to make up a doggy bag presents itself. Human remains, even those exposed to the air by the natural degradation of the burial plot itself are best left where they are, though fragments of marble from grave markers and rusted coffin nails are of course fair game.

Altar Beasts

A relatively involved use of found items, such as the aforementioned feathers and animal bones, is in the creation of an Altar Beast. This is an empowered thought form specifically designed to protect your ritual space from outside forces that would seek to disrupt its day to day workings. The actual make up of the creature depends largely on the materials gathered by the necromant and their ingenuity in sculpting a viable likeness of the tulpa in the mundane world. The entity itself is then named, programmed with the laws that govern its function and finally birthed by the magickian through a process of intense visualisation and repeated applications of the necromant's own blood.

While it does not need to be a work of art in the classical sense, the necrotic modelling wire and ersatz cadaver creature that forms under the magickian's fingers should be a viable representation of the initial idea, and reflect its purpose as watchful guardian of the necromancer's working laboratory. It goes without saying that this physical body is but an anchor point in the material realm for an entity wished into being in such a way, and not animate. It will never actually get up off of the altar and run around with a kitchen knife and a tiny little hockey mask, more's the pity, yet this in no way diminishes its effectiveness as a viable last line of defence when dealing with the unreal reality in which a conduit of the death current operates.

A related methodology presents itself for those who either lack the skill required to create a tulpa, or who prefer to work exclusively with the spirits of the recently departed instead. In this respect the altar beast serves not so much as a focal point for the creation of a synthetic astral being, but instead a portal through which an ancestor can be incited to return and commence its silent vigil over the necromant and their family. The magickian utilises items and trinkets belonging to the person to be contacted in this way during the creation process, and programs the sculpture by overlaying it with feelings and memories relating to them while they were alive. It is, however, not to be seen as a prison for the resident spirit; if mistreated or disrespected they will no doubt abandon their task at the first available opportunity, perhaps even turning on the necromancer in the process.

Depending upon your location and time of year, many different plants and flowers can be found growing wildly within the cemetery walls as well, adding to its otherworldly bounty. This is especially true at the usually poorly maintained edges where no one really goes unless they need to pee. Roses long since left to grow as they wish vie for space with numerous forms of ivy and holly, punctuated by the occasional thistle and poppy. Plus acorns, conkers and seed pods, leaves and fallen branches all drop in abundance, especially in autumn and early winter. This adds a distinct rhythm to the interactions between a necromant and their favourite graveyard similar in many ways to the pagan wheel of the year.

Those seeking wood to craft a wand or cut for runes can do far worse than look to the trees in their local cemetery, especially the ones growing out of a grave or tomb. Indeed, any plant that has germinated above a burial and then laid roots down within the remains of the dead becomes a natural conduit for the death current. When taken in concert with their obvious ties to the forces of nature as well, we see a unique blending of life and unlife within a single material, and an obvious choice for the discerning mage looking to exploit both forces to their fullest potential.

It goes without saying that bringing ritual implements and other associated trinkets within the boundaries of most inner-city graveyards is almost impossible during the busy daylight hours. Access to these spaces after dark is also limited, and as such the cover of night is not usually available for even the most daring magickian to take advantage of either. This should not actually be an issue, however, as no tools are required when working within the cemetery itself.

The gateways to the underworld yawn wide in the places of burial, and as such are capable of providing more than enough empowerment to achieve any given entropic goal. Thus the land beneath the necromancer's feet becomes the most valuable treasure of all.

Gateway Meditation

There will come a time when every necromant inevitably finds themselves in search of guidance from the other side of the veil. When this need arises a field trip of sorts is undertaken, involving the magickian approaching the dead on their own soil for help and advice. Devoid of the regular tools and trappings of their art, the necromancer is forced to face the steely gaze of the discarnate entities who populate that sacred space empty-handed, gambling that their strength of will alone will prove strong enough to see them through the trial that lies ahead.

All the necromant requires to begin a gateway meditation is a shady spot under a large tree, preferably one which sprouted from a burial and that sits far enough away from the general flow of traffic through the cemetery that they remain undisturbed. The magickian then sits with their back pressed against the cool bark of the corpse-gorged trunk and, while resting their palms gently on the soil at its roots, begins to meditate on the dual nature of life and unlife. As their concentration builds they will perceive the world slowing down, and an icy chill creeping up their spine. At this point, the necromancer is channelling the very death current itself, and sitting on the cusp of two very different worlds. Shades will start to gather, questions can be asked and answers gained, before the spell is broken and normal consciousness sluggishly reasserts itself.

The more the necromancer experiments with this altered reality, the more adept they will become at channelling the death current, as well as dealing with the denizens of the unseen world. During these experiments there is a very real possibility of the magickian shifting from sticky fingered interloper to honoured guest within the cemetery grounds, their resonance with the icy flow of entropic power growing until they become a true mage-priest of the dead. Theirs is now the mantle of go-between for the real and unreal worlds, and a symbiotic relationship forms with the spirits who offered them the chance of such a chilling rebirth in the first place.

As this article highlights, there is much more to modern necromancy than simply digging up the dead and stealing their skulls. At its unbeating heart it can be best viewed as working with the essence of place as opposed to the physical remains of those who have long since passed beyond the veil. While many less enlightened people will sneer at the idea of walking out of a cemetery with a bag of soil or sack of animal bones, such actions are undertaken with reverence and clarity by the true necromant, who realises that there is little real value in desecrating human remains. Thankfully, none of the aforementioned treasures of the grave are particularly tricky to acquire once you have found a quiet corner to begin your work, and doing so should have little or no effect on the ecosystem of the cemetery whatsoever.

A final note of warning, however; be mindful of those coming to visit the graves of the recently deceased. Odds are your reverence for the undertaking that brought you to walk amongst the dead in the first place would be of little comfort to them should they find you with your fingers in their newly planted family tree. Remember, as with any other source of magickal materials, once you find a viable burial plot that is capable of providing for your needs long term it is best to do nothing that might jeopardize your ability to harvest there. Stupidity and waste are not the virtues of a competent necromancer after all, nor do they bode well for your continued survival within a very dangerous paradigm.

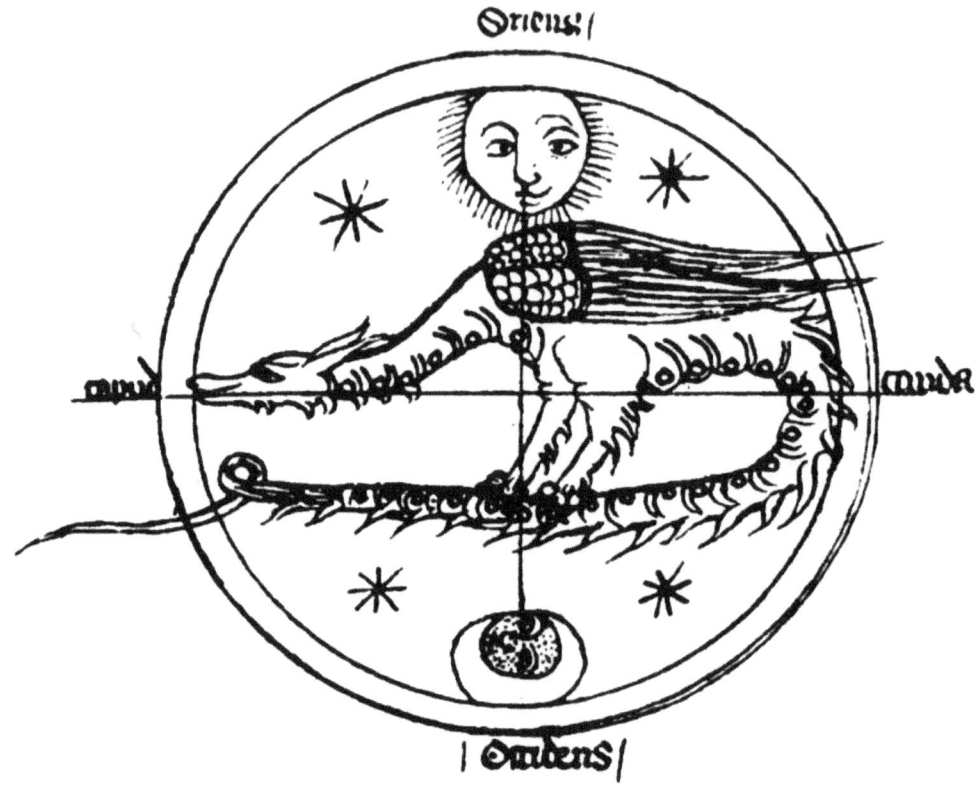

Michael Scot: The Life of a True Magician

by Eldred Hieronymus Wormwood

In the course of my studies into the history of magic in the western world I have come again and again onto a near mythical figure from the late 12th and early 13th century. Michael Scot, mentioned extensively in both historic accounts and folk legends, appears as an alchemist and early scientist whose work has long been overlooked in the modern era.

There are few magicians in history who are the equal of the 13th century Scottish "necromancer" and alchemist Michael Scot. From the slanderous fictions told about him after his death by Roger Bacon and Albertus Magnus, his being mentioned by name in Dante's *Inferno*, and the dedication to him at the front of Fibonacci's work *Liber Ababci*, Scot is without parallel in the history of science and magic. The tales that have arisen in the centuries since his death, particularly in the border counties of Scotland - the place of his birth and rumoured death, are born primarily out of historic slanders and the wistful mythologizing of his ancestor Sir Walter Scott.

Despite much misinformation over the centuries, Michael Scot was a real man; his deeds and studies leave behind a fascinating tale of one man's quest throughout Europe to discover the natural order of the world, the secrets of ancient cultures, and the ways of their masters of craft.

Born ostensibly in the Scottish border counties in 1170, Scot is believed to have studied at Oxford sometime in the early 13th century before departing to France, where he would take up the study of mathematics at the proto-university that would become the Sorbonne at Paris. After some years of study in France, the wanderlust that would be a hallmark of Scot's career came again and Scot travelled south, first to Spain and ultimately finding himself in Sicily at the court of the Holy Roman Emperor Fredrick II.

The earliest record of Scot's life and studies dates from August of 1217 in Toledo Spain, where Scot had just completed the translation from Arabic into Latin of the first work to present a non-Ptolemaic astronomical system, al-Bitruji's *Alpetragius*. During this period Scot took part in the school of translation at Toledo, and became acquainted with the works of Aristotle through the Arabic commentaries of Averroes.

Here Scot would undertake one of, if not the very first, translation of Averroes (Ibn Rushd) to Latin from the original Arabic. His translations of Aristotle's *Historia animalium*, *De caelo*, and the *De anima* would later be published at the considerable expense of the Holy Roman Emperor Fredrick II.

In 1220 he would travel southwest, spending time in Palermo and then on to Sicily and be made the tutor and court astrologer of Fredrick II, King of Sicily and the future Holy Roman Emperor. Here he began to compile a work *Liber Introductorius maior in astrologiam* ("Great Book on the introduction to Astrology"), that would be created as a kind of encyclopedia for the Emperor. Broken into three books, "*Liber quatuor distinctionum*" ("Book of four distinctions"), "*Liber particularis*" ("Singular Book"), with the "*De mirabilibus mundi*" ("Marvels of the World"), and the "*Liber physiognomiae*" ("Book of physiognomy") the work presented Fredrick with a reference guide to understanding the nature of the world and its astrological functions. It included various alchemical and divinatory tracts, particularly in "*Liber Physiognomiae*", a work on the art of physiognomy.

"*Physionomia is the science of nature by whose insinuation one sufficiently skilled in it recognizes the differences of animals, and the vices and virtues of persons of all sorts.*" -Liber physiognomiae, Introduction, (translated by Lynn Thorndike)

During this period at court Scot would be given a wide berth of investigatory intellectual freedom from both his patron and the Papal See. A hallmark of the Court of Fredrick II was that, despite Papal edicts to the contrary, Fredrick allowed full human autopsies for the first time, giving Scot unprecedented access to the inner workings of the human body, much of which is described in "*Liber Physiognomiae*".

Scot's feats and tasks during this time at court made him renown throughout the continent. His intellectual and mathematic accomplishments were widely known in his era, and the methodology he would undertake in his study of the natural world and its underpinning mathematical functions would set him far apart from his contemporaries.

In 1227 the mathematician Leonardo Fibonacci dedicated the second and revised edition of his groundbreaking work *Liber Abaci* to Scot, giving the dedication -

" You have written to me, my Lord Michael Scotus, supreme philosopher, that I should transcribe for you the book on numbers which I composed some time since. Wherefore, acceding to your demand and going over it carefully, I have revised it in your honor and for the use of many others. In this revision I have added some necessary matters and cut some superfluidities. In it I have given the complete doctrine of numbers according to the method of the Hindus, which method I have chosen as superior to others in this science . . .

To make the doctrine more apparent, I have divided the book into fifteen chapters, so that the reader may more readily find whatever he is looking for. Furthermore, if in this work inadequacy or defect is found, I submit that to your emendation." - L. Thorndike, 1965, IV, [pp.34-35]

Leonardo's concepts of mathematics were laid out in the works of Al-Khwarizmi and Abu Kamil Shuja, both authors whom Scot had translated while in Toledo. Scot and Fibonacci likely became acquainted as fellow members of the Court of Fredrick and each would come to represent primary conduits of Arabic mathematics and sciences to European thinking. The possibility exists that their relationship may have predated their time together at Court, as both learned men would crisscross Spain in their research and studies.

It has been suggested by various academics that Scot was responsible for the sequence of calculations that

ORIGINAL NOTE OF A CONSULTATION OF MICHAEL SCOT AT BOLOGNA
IN THE YEAR 1221
(From Gonville and Caius College MS. of the 13th century)

led to what is now commonly called the "Fibonacci Sequence." It was Leonardo's *Liber Abaci* that introduced the Hindo-Arabic numeral system into Western culture and thus paved the way for the birth of modern mathematic research during the Renaissance.

During these Sicily years Scot would become familiar with the vast cross current of cultures happening in the Mediterranean. Arabic, Christian and Jewish societies intermingled and gave birth to much of the scholarship and mystical thinking that would be the foundation of the coming Renaissance.

At some point in his career Scot must have taken up holy orders and been ordained as a priest. It was in Sicily that he would twice be offered a Bishopric by the seated Pope. In 1223 he was offered the role of the Archbishop of Cashel in Ireland by Pope Honorius III and later he would be offered the Bishopric of Canterbury in 1227 by Pope Gregory IX. He declined the Cashel seat with the dismissive that he did "not speak Irish", likely avoiding the Pope's attempts to remove Scot from the ear of the Emperor.

According to J. Wood Brown there is an account of a story told by the chronicler Salimbene that the Emperor asked Scot one day to determine the distance of the coelum (roof's height) in the hall of the palace where they stood talking.

"The calculation having been made and the result given, Frederick took occasion to send Scot on a distant journey, and, while he was away, the proportions of the room were slightly but sufficiently altered. On his return the Emperor led him where they had been before and asked that he should repeat his solution of the problem. Scot unhesitatingly affirmed that a change had taken place - either the floor was higher or the coelum lower than before: an answer which made all men marvel at his skill."
- J.W. Brown

In the late 1220s, under Fredrick's instruction, Scot began to travel again throughout Europe with his recently published (under Fredrick's patronage) translations of Aristotle's *Historia animalium*, a zoological natural history that would be later mostly paraphrased in the Emperor's own work *De Arte Venandi cum Avibu* ("The Art of Hunting with Birds"), published shortly after Scot's death sometime in the late 1230s.

Much of the legend surrounding Scot's life as a necromancer, alchemist and wizard would be seeded during this late period of his travels. His interactions with various academic institutions, the visual impression he must have made upon those mostly northern Europeans who saw him now aged in his Mediterranean/Arabic influenced forms of dress, and the accent he had acquired throughout his life of exploration left a rather motley impression.

The last days of Scot's life are not well known with any verifiable accounts. He is mentioned as having recently passed in the topical literature of the early 1240s, and within the century after his death the vast Michael Scot mythologies would begin to emerge. In the border counties of his birth in southern Scotland they would speak of his return late in life, living under the prophetic knowledge of his own impending death by a stone falling from the sky only to be killed when removing his protective metal cap during Church service. Perhaps more a Scottish warning about the Church than any factual account of Scot's death?

+ + +

As with many great historic thinkers Scot would have his detractors. Albertus Magnus and Roger Bacon would both in their time take the opportunity to slander and libel Michael Scot. Accusations of charlatanism and sorcery abounded and the image that began to emerge of Scot as a formidable wizard whose dealings with the devil were those of a magician capable of binding the devil to his word, would take hold throughout the Middle Ages.

In Sir Walter Scott (1805) there is a tale of Michael Scot, now returned to living in a stone tower on the banks of the river Ettrick, near Selkirk in Scotland, having learned of a nearby witch with whom he took the chance to visit. Upon a distracted moment of dropping his wand the witch, who had feigned a simple woman's life until that instant, seized it and used it to turn Scot into the glamour of a hare. After being chased by his own hounds before he could shake off the glamour Scot got his revenge by casting a spell upon the witch that trapped her in a dance that would ensorcel any who entered her home.

It was said as well that Scot had tested a demon's strength by making him divide Eildon Hill into its three distinctive cones, where only one peak had formerly been, and to weave rope from the sand of a beach. Dante and Boccaccio both present Michael Scot as a dead wizard residing in the Eighth Circle of Hell - reserved for "sorcerers, astrologers, and false prophets".

In many ways the myth of the legendary Scot would come to overshadow the truth of the real man and his quest for knowledge. Unlike St. Cyprian, for whom little verifiable evidence exists to confirm he was anything more than a fictional fabrication, Scot left a wide paper trail behind him.

Though Scot's own works contain what would be now referred to as magical operations, alchemical recipes and practical sorceries a large body of pseudo-Scotus material later came into existence in the centuries after his death. Mostly cribbed works of grimoiric magic, ceremonial ritual operations and the like these works would be attributed to Scot much as they would later be attributed to Faust and St Cyprian.

+ + +

When we look at the arc of Scot's life it is the periods he spent in Toledo that seem to have the widest effect on his work as both a translator and scholar. Here his introduction to the works of Arabic writers and translators would coexist within the birthplace of Hebraic Kabbalist philosophies. Scot, it is said, employed a Jewish convert to Christianity called Andrew as a translator of Hebrew during his time in Toledo.

It has been suggested in a study of Scot's work on the phenomenon of "multiple rainbows", a property of light only understood by modern physics, that Michael Scot may have had contact with the Tuareg people of the Sahara desert. In Scot's work he predicts that beyond the visible light of the primary and secondary rainbow there must exist at least two other rainbow patterns of light. This phenomena was only verified in the late 20th century.

While we have little in the way of surviving accounts of his days in Toledo, the current of great thinkers and translators under the patronage of Archbishop Raymond of Toledo (founder of the Toledo School of Translators), the influx of Jewish and North African travelers, and the general multicultural atmosphere of Spain during this period had a lasting impression upon Scot and his work.

Scot's reading and translation of works by Avicenna and Averroes as well as his study and eventual translations of the Arabic versions of Aristotle and the many commentaries of the Arabs upon them led him to create his singular work of alchemy the *Ars Alchemie*.

Known to us from three existent manuscripts (two of which contain potentially spurious additional material), *Ars Alchemie* was designed to reveal the "Secret of the Philosophers". Detailed descriptions of metals and their relationship to planets, examinations of both classes for their inherent nature, recipes and instructions for the transformation of "Venus into the sun", of mercury into silver, and of lead into gold, and the nature of salts are among the other main topics discussed in the treatise.

The "*Lumen Luminum*" portion of the *Ars Alchemie* was believed by Thorndike to have been a translation or abridgment of the earlier work by the same name that is ascribed to Al-Razi. Containing an exquisite description of an alchemical study of salts and their properties, it is found together with a rather short text, "*Experimenta necromantica*", that appears with regard to Scot's possibly pseudo literature.

It is in the *Ars Alchemie*, whether in translation or personal text from experimentation, that Scot reveals the often overlooked depth of a complex form of entheogenic drug use among the Arabic alchemists present and past in Scot's world. Here we find methods of chemical distillation and infusion that merge biological incubators with a profound knowledge of chemical extracts and their properties.

The second portion of the *Ars Alchemia*, "*Liber Dedali*" (possibly the only existent record of a believed lost classical work *Dedalus grecus*), Scot speaks of the creation of a salt alkaloid intended to give visions of complex beings and to reveal nature for its "true self". His remarkable understanding of the ways in which chemical properties could yield changes in the physiologic and psychological body places him more than a handful of centuries ahead of contemporary science.

In the "*Liber Dedali*" Scot instructs the alchemist in the preparation of a powder derived from toads that brings "fantastic visions". The primary process of creating this powder is to fill a container with living toads in a wine and salt solution one creates beforehand. I give the text in question translated from Scot's (admittedly rather awkward) Latin with my commentary in parentheses:

"Total yield of the operation/procedure of boiled/fermented/processed solution is the same as represented by the subject/initial group/value, based on the quantity of the sample area (3.5).

After grinding it with caution, use only fresh (red/not congealed) human blood, to the amount of 3.3. Commit/use a Gutta (a device used in alchemy or medicine for accuracy, resembling the Gutta used in the architrave of Doric Classical Architecture... a small water-repelling, cone-shaped projection.)

Additionally, you may use a pinch of sulphur, 3.5 of talc and grind them white with the blood and salt. After they have dried safely, transmute them with heat from the Sun or an oven. Ensure full drying by stirring with mortar and pestle. It may be kept, & used when need arises. Apply heat from a fire to activate, taking care not to scatter the solution by use of bellows.

The quantity (unknown value) of solution of not more than 5 pounds is removed from the heat of the fire to be thrown in to salt/brine-water for a long time (between 45 and 75 minutes) then this is the best compound.

Take five (black) toads and put them in a vase (previously filled with wine, which reacts to the toad's venom and results in a powerful chemical transformation, after the toad poisons itself and dies), to prepare them to receive Victorious Rose (unknown plant) or (unknown kind of Arabic plant), and a dried solution of ground Christmas Rose/Black Hellebore; also a mixture of brine-water in equal amounts as the previously-mentioned dried solution; also with ammoniated salt measuring 3.5, ground in a hole, and dried with urine from nine pigs, from the same field.

The resultant "dust" does wonders, and cannot help to. It transmutes everything into perfect clarity, as the clarity of the Moon. It completely changes the perspective, as Mars is said to do. If you have imbibed the dust at a measurement of 3.2, and drink, based on your own perspective, you will find life-spirit which transcends and far outweighs the effort or cost you have put into the making of this product.

You may use the dust as substitute for salt, as is done by Southern Spaniards, in Northern Italy, and in Belgium (Roman province of Gallia Belgica Muide).

Do not document your observations, while under the influence, though you may record them after the effects have worn off. I have unsatisfactorily (in a pale imitation of the experience) written down my feelings (while under the influence) in the past.

While undergoing the effects of the compound, the N O W is separated from the T H E N/later.

Use ammoniated aluminium-sulfate on the seeds in pre-heated salt-brine-water. Return the water to double the previous temperature. Then congeal/harden the substance in wax. Here, do not doubt the process: you are well on your way to mastering the final product.

After this, place the waxed product between two saucers and place in a glass vessel. I implore you to close your mouth. Wash away the salt. After a day, cut it in half, using (Venetian) Ceruse (Spirits of Saturn): it will then be hardened and completed, able to withstand great temperatures.

Before halving the product, ensure that calcination has fully taken effect, and that you have introduced the Ceruse only at the right time (after the sweating, washing off of salt, & the passage of a day). The product will appear white.

This calcination process (method unknown/ related to Alchemal Mercury), and should not have additional steps added to it. This you will see, when you lose the whiteness of the product, and can only perfect by trial and error.

If you have allowed too much water to remain in the product, you will find out in the Spring. If, however, you undergo the Springtime, and it works, you should repeat the same experiment in the same way.

Archelaus (Ionian philosopher) discovered his truths through this product. You, too, may reduce the product to ash and understand the same truths.

Then, take the final product, after it has set the appropriate amount of time, and use as much fresh juice as comes from the diameter of the Hellebore, as much as you dare, and place it into an unused vessel, containing toads. Let them drink for nine days. Mix the ammoniated product with pig urine, dry and grind. You will have Wisdom, and you will be of the third level of eight. Rejoice.

Even Alchemists who deal with red clay and red earth - dust buffoons, all of them - were able to achieve success by following this recipe. What they possessed, few people knew.

This type of knowledge derives straight from the blessed God Almighty, which is the first cause of all things. All that is needful may be acquired, by following this recipe, as these men did, I say to you firmly. Thus, they kept silent as to the recipe, and as to the essence of the product, and sold only regular salts in the open."

- Michael Scot, "Liber Dedali" from *Ars Alchemie*, (12th century)

+ + +

Clearly this text shows that the use of entheogenic material was well known to alchemists at least by the 13th century, possibly (depending on the source of the "Liber Denali") from antiquity. Michael Scot's detailed descriptions of a "dust" or powder that can be consumed and smoked that will yield "fantastic visions" and allow for the human mind to expand into new realms of knowing reveals a profound understanding of both chemistry and human psychology.

While the folktales of Scot give him fantastic powers of spell casting, conjuration, divination and prophecy, most of these later legends were intended as slander, meant to diminish his reputation among thinkers of that age after his death. Yet while they were able to diminish his name in the history of science it was also these fantastic stories that have kept his name in the mouths of mankind even till today.

Yet as Thorndike has long shown, the history of science and magic is one of twins; born of the same mother they evolved over millenia only to be separated in recent centuries "post-rationale". They are cut of the same cloth, that which seeks out knowledge and dares authority to question the very fabric of being. Scot was in many ways a predecessor to Newton, whose own alchemical past was muted by his 19th & 20th century publishers. Scot's life of travels reflect the imaginary Iberian adventures of St Cyprian set more than two centuries after Scot's death.

If we can judge a man by the enemies he keeps, holding out Roger Bacon, Albertus Magnus, Dante Algheri, and Boccaio gives one the impression of a man whose very existence and the depth of his knowledge of natural magic struck fear into lesser thinkers of later generations. That power to elicit wonder and fear at the scope of one's search for knowledge and the nature of reality is ultimately the work of a true wizard.

Michael Scot was possibly the greatest thinker of his age. Sought out by Emperors and Popes, reviled by lesser men whose timid thinking was overshadowed by Scot's brilliance, consulted by the geniuses of his era to check their sums and examine their translations, he lived the life of a true magician. Seeking to know how the world works, from the smith's hammer to the alchemist's crucible, from the priest's gowns to the sufi's robes. It is this quest of a lifetime spent in pursuit of knowing that is the hallmark of a great magician, and the tales of his fictitious adventures in crude sorcery are outshone by his actual feats of profound human knowledge.

When we consider the founders of esoteric thought over the past several millennia these men and women were roundly scientists. They sought out a greater understanding of the shape of the universe and obstinately defied the authorities prescribed cosmology in favor of one of forbidden knowledge.

Many of the later thinkers of early science, from Ibn Razi to Paracelsus, from Fibbonanci to Newton, were alchemists and necromancers looking for answers to the big questions. They sought out secrets much in the way of an experimental scientist, in fact they created the very framework on which modern science rests. By looking both to historic texts as a guide and to physical experimentation to provide positive truths they questioned the dogmatic schematic of the world presented by the church and crown.

These seekers after truth traveled the world, learned new languages, spoke to, and importantly listened to as wide a breadth of humanity as they could in order to understand how others perceived reality. They harvested the useful bits of information hidden within each culture, from the knowing texts of learned men to that whispered knowledge of the folk, and mixed these ideas together to form an overarching universal understanding of reality. They translated foreign texts into common languages, bringing the results of their research into the light of contemporary readership.

Michael Scot stood at the edge of two cultures, the Arabic Berber Caliphate and the Holy Roman Empire, at a period in which the intermingling of these cultures was giving birth to much of the later centuries explorations of mystical knowledge. Kabbalah was being formed, ceremonial texts that were derived from eastern and more obscure sources were being codified, dangerous experiments with a vast array of chemicals and physical states were being explored.

This seeking after the unknown to grasp at the fabric of reality was, and remains, true magic. Doing things others fear in order to understand what lies beyond the edge of human knowledge. Exploring the world in which we exist and questioning the fabric of what is generally understood to be the boundaries of reality. Going out to explore the world in person instead of relying on the tales of others with which to derive your opinions of the world and its boundaries.

The modern magician is presented with a vast array of information in the form of rare manuscripts and published grimoires, as well as an ocean of contemporary magical published material that ranges from the purely fictional to serious occult research. Yet much of that readership are merely armchair magicians, who read the works of others and yet do no research of their own, can not or will not perform the experiments (i.e. rituals/spells) required to understand and verify those work written in the vast literature of occult science and art.

Throughout history the true magicians are those whose work leaves ripples on the fabric of history, producing original and apocryphal texts, giving birth to legend and folktale whose true nature makes it hard to grasp. Their actions leave a wake in time, providing all possible futures with the essence of their working.

Michael Scot truly understood reality in a way few men of his age could begin to grasp. His research continues to be verified even in the modern era of contemporary science. His legend is the stuff of folktale, not invalid for its resonance in society, though fantastic in its hagiographic absurdness.

Much scholarship into the works of Michael Scot, particularly in translating the bulk of his work into English, remains to be done. Thorndike and various others picked at the edges of these works, translating in excerpt as I have done above, but it remains a task for contemporary scholars to dig into the material and provide a critical analysis of the original manuscripts we have access to today. I, for one, would wholeheartedly support such a project.

References:

Michael Scot in Spain - Charles Haskins, Harvard University 1918

The Texts of Michael Scot's Ars Alchemie - S. H. Thomson 1938

The Life and Legend of Michael Scot - J W Brown 1897

The Liber Introductorius Of Michael Scot - Glenn Michael Edwards 1978

Michael Scot: Myth and Polymath - Tom Hubbard 2006

Michael Scot - Lynn Thorndike 1968

A History of Magic and Experimental Science Vol 1 & 2, L Thorndike 1929-34

On the Origin of the Fibonacci Sequence - T.C. Scotta & P. Marketosc 2014

Michael Scot and the Four Rainbows - Scott, Tony 2017

The Picatrix Decan Art Project
J Swofford

I HAVE BEEN fascinated with the *Picatrix* since I first heard about it on Poke Runyon's *Hermetic Hour* podcast in the autumn of 2011. I don't remember now when the actual episode was posted but that was when I heard it, sitting in an airport late at night. He described it as the manual *par excellence* for the making and use of images and talismanic magic. It seemed to me the perfect intersection of my artistic activities and my interest in the occult and I immediately bought a copy of the Greer and Warnock translation of the Latin *Picatrix*. I have been digging through it ever since and still feel like there is so, so much yet to discover.

Part of what I find so intriguing about the *Picatrix* is that throughout the book it almost taunts the reader by saying that much of what is written as instruction is deliberately in code and obscured in cryptic language while at the same time laying out that instruction in beautiful, poetic imagery that hints at deeper mysteries. It is riddles inside riddles, "seemingly placed by accident".

In the summer of 2017 I began an art project to explore one small part of the *Picatrix*, the description of the decans of the signs in Book 2, chapter 11. They seemed straightforward enough. But, of course I found that they were much deeper and more profound than I had imagined. It is one of those classic situations in which I found that the more I studied, the less I knew or was sure about. That is not to say, however, that I learned nothing. I found the project enlightening and empowering and I am proud of what I was able to accomplish.

One of the important things I learned in the making of this project was that the images describe the ruling planet in a particular sign. When the *Picatrix*'s descriptions of the decans begins with "the first face of Aries *is* Mars", it is giving us a clue that we are reading a description of an image of the planet Mars. This is distinct from a Martial spirit and is important when we empower these images as talismans. The timing of such an operation is best when the planet is ascending in the face in question. And when it is, here is what it looks like, what it feels like.

Before I get too much deeper into the philosophic considerations of the *Picatrix* decans I would like to talk a bit about how the images were made. The first thing I would like to note is that they are photographs and were originally intended to be photographs. Each one was shot on a copy stand with my digital SLR camera. Everything in each picture is an object, an image cut out of a book or magazine, or razor cut construction paper.

I did not make them in any particular order. As I finished one, I would pick the next as the mood struck me. Nor did I pay attention to planetary correspondences in terms of day or hour. I let myself be guided by my intuition. Literarily I was guided mainly by the Greer and Warnock Latin *Picatrix* with a fair dose of Austin Coppock's *36 Faces*. I avoided most of the other writings about the decans including Agrippa, Ibn Ezra, and correspondences to the Rider-Waite or Thoth tarot decks.

I wanted to make this project an examination of the *Picatrix* itself and so I wanted that book to be the main inspiration for the images.

And while I do believe the decans are aspects of the planets, I also believe they represent other mythological characters. The identities I feel fairly confident about are from Greek mythology but there are reasons to believe that some of the others will turn out to be from other pantheons. I continue to do research in this line of thinking. For me the art-making process was instrumental in these conceptual connections. In general, I find art-making to be an excellent way to meditate deeply on a particular idea. It becomes a method of research in which the unconscious and intuitive parts of the mind can be leveraged to their most useful.

Here are three examples of images from the series. The text of the passage is from the Greer & Warnock translation of the Latin *Picatrix*. My analyses are my own.

3rd Decan of Aries

There rises in the third face of Aries, a restless man, holding in his hands a gold bracelet, wearing red clothing, who wishes to do good but is not able to do it. This is a face of subtlety and subtle mastery and new things and instruments and similar things.

The keyword for this decan is compulsion. This is what "subtlety and subtle mastery" means in this context, that one has succumbed to a powerful influence without even noticing. As a Venusian face of a Martial sign it is manifest as Cupid or Eros, whose amorous arrows could move even the gods to outrageous acts of folly. I have depicted the restless man as a faceless red devil who holds a large hoop of gold around him. A cherubic cupid shoots him in the heart with a pink arrow and he is subsequently bound through the eyes of a smiling face and pulled into flames below. This is an image of a person seeing the wrong choice and choosing it anyway due to some kind of compulsion: love or duty or something else. Our restless man is, therefore, an image of suffering.

As a talisman this image moves others despite their best intentions. It can also make one aware of how they are themselves moved by unconscious desires and compulsions.

1st Decan of Cancer

There rises in the first face of Cancer a man whose fingers and head are distorted and slanted, and his body is similar to a horse's body; his feet are white, and he has fig leaves on his body. This is a face of instruction, knowledge, love, subtlety and mastery.

This decan is a depiction of Chiron the centaur, legendary instructor of many Greek heroes. The planetary ruler of this decan is Venus and the fig is representative of her. The fig leaf has connotations as the covering of the genitals of Adam and Eve before they were aware of their sexuality. Placing a mass of these leaves where his legs meet his body references this. Adam named all things in the world and strengthens the connotations of knowledge and instruction. I believe the description of his feet being white is meant to elevate Chiron above the centaurs who were reported to be brutish and crass. This represents the influence of Venus again in the form of beautification and refinement. We find a third instance of Venus's influence when we consider the paternal relationship that existed between tutors and their charges in the Classic world.

In the passage from the *Picatrix* it is said that his head and hands are distorted and slanted. Elsewhere in the *Picatrix* we are told that this is code for aspects of death, and in this way this is an image of an undead character. Chiron is the injured healer, one who sacrifices themselves so that another may live. Through his sacrifice he is made immortal.

As a talisman this image is one for learning, finding knowledge, and forming a relationship with a teacher. On a related note it has connotations of immortality through the transmission of ideas and educational lineage.

1st Decan of Virgo

There rises in the first face of virgo a young girl covered with an old woolen cloth, and in her hand is a pomegranate. This is a face of sowing, plowing, the germination of plants, of gathering grapes, and of good living.

This decan was the first to give me a clue that these decans may represent figures from Greek myth. It seemed clear to me that a young girl wearing an old woolen cloth and holding a pomegranate indicated Persephone, the Greek goddess who was abducted by the god of the Underworld to be his wife. Persephone is a complex goddess. On the one hand she is the goddess of sprouting new growth and the return of spring after winter. On the other hand, as wife to Hades, the god of the Underworld, she was also queen of that realm and ruled over the dead and the depths of the earth. In the stories that I am familiar with, after Persephone is abducted her mother Demeter, goddess of fruit and grain, searches for her and ignores the fruits of the earth, allowing fallow winter to descend on the earth. Hades eventually agrees to let Persephone return to the surface world but tempts her to eat of a pomegranate, which she does, by which she is bound to return to the Underworld for part of the year. By interpreting the old woolen cloth as a sort of burial shroud, the description of this decan in the *Picatrix* includes all of her motifs: youth, a pomegranate, and the sowing and growth of plants.

The *Picatrix* tells us that the color appropriate to this decan is "a mixture of red and gold". I was unsure whether this meant orange, or red and yellow together but unmixed. I chose to land somewhere in the middle with an incomplete mix of red and yellow into a streaky plane that is more orange than either of the two colors.

The main figure described in this passage of the *Picatrix* is near the top of the composition. She is a young woman with her eyes and nose cut to resemble a skull. Her eyes are cut in the shape of a lidded eye, as opposed to an eye socket, to represent vision beyond the mundane, a sort of far, spiritual vision. This is in contrast to the circular shape cut from the eyes of the faces at the bottom of the composition. The round eyes represent the coins on the eyes of the dead in ancient burial ceremonies.

In this image I wanted to reference both the qualities of growth as well as death. To that end I put three spirits at the bottom of the composition, one a skull and two eyeless faces, and four stalks of spearmint and a carpet of mint leaves. The stalks of mint appear to be growing through the eyes of the two spirit faces.

This represents the intimate connection between the spirits of this decan and the fecundity of the earth.

As a talisman this image is one that calls upon the powers of the spirits of the deep earth. These are spirits of growth and are strongly connected to one's ancestors. This image reminds us of the connection between loved ones who have passed away and the gifts they bestow on the living for their continued progress.

As a practical tool for a creative magician the decan images have several potential uses. Among some examples, first, as individual tokens they can be printed and then suffumigated, anointed, and empowered to exude their influence according to the will of the practitioner – in short, made into a talisman in the classic sense of the *Picatrix*. The printed image can be used in ritual combined with herbs, words, sigils, or other magical elements for all manner of purposes.

Second, taken together like a deck of cards they can be used as a sortilege divination system, the talismanic connotations serving as the divinatory meaning.

Third, they can be used as reference to the influences of the individual planets in the decan they rule. By this I mean that each image conveys the emotional and magical influences of the decan and so can be used to get a feel for the decan. The decans were once a timekeeping device, each one rising with the Sun for approximately ten days. The images of the decans then give a sense of some of the astrological weather prevalent in their time of year.

Magical image making is essentially an act of distilling an emotion or intent down to a simple picture. This is where the magic is, in that distillation. Just as Austin Osman Spare distilled his intent into a sigil made of the consonants of his statement of his will, the *Picatrix* gives us images to distill the astrological influences of each of the decans. Part of the power of image-making is in its ability to convey nuanced information in the abstract. An image, when done well, is a way of understanding without intellectualizing.

In some ways the *Picatrix* defies understanding. It is deliberately cryptic and obscure. I have come to understand that as one digs into any one particular part of the *Picatrix*, the less one really knows about it. It continues to be an unending source of spiritual and intellectual pleasure.

AZTEC SOLAR MAGICK: BLOOD AND GOLD
ERICA FREVEL

CULTIC USAGES OF GOLD IN MEXICO

No single Aztec deity was exclusively associated with gold, but all exhibited a connection with solar attributes: power, wealth and war. In fact many of the darker spirits and those of the underworld were honored with golden idols and ceremonial priests decked in gold. Tezcatlipoca, the darkest of the primordial gods, was offered gold bracelets and strands of gold bells. Contemporary devotions to Santa Muerte count gold amongst her many robes. While this may seem contradictory, the Aztec mindset did not draw strict lines between bright solar and dark death energies. All energy seemed to stem from the sun, materially and metaphorically. The sun was not relegated to a singular god with a fixed identity. Each celestial house the sun journeys through sees the sun donning a new spirit mask or manifestation.

Daily, the Morning Sun became the Night Sun and descended into the underworld where he interacted with the Lords of Night, perhaps becoming one himself. Most deities were interconnected because the source of divinity lay not in the distinct deity but in the sacred movement-change in the cosmos which was interfaced by the mask-spirit of teotl. The movement-change of death and rejuvenation was of particular interest to the Aztec cult. Gold was applied ritually to both sides of the spectrum of life and death.

Gold was one of the most expensive and precious metals in Mesoamerica. There are an average amount of gold deposits in Central and South America, and the deposits were rather accessible to miners. Gold is associated with the sun not simply because the sun is the most important or precious celestial body, but also due to an elaborate spiritual connection between the "Excrement of the Sun" and the "People of the Sun". The heightened level of spiritual dedication and intricate artistry of Mesoamerican gold cult objects is without equal. A visit to any major museums' Mesoamerican collection makes this fact self-evident.

Gold was mined alongside many other minerals and gems in mineral-rich Western Mexico where metallurgy began to develop a bit after 600 AD within smaller communities. Larger empires in central and eastern Mexican states grew steadily alongside their cult need for gold. Often, common people simply searched for their own gold bits to suit their individual needs. An effective system of hand panning was used in the rivers to collect small chunks of gold that were typically ground down to dust or melted down and used to make jewelry. Simple bellows and crucible were fashioned of thick reed found on the banks of the same rivers in which they panned for gold. Later in the classical period, goldsmithing reached its height as a perfected craft even more advanced than those of Europe at the time. Finding it much easier to work than dense jade, which was another spiritually precious substance, goldsmiths became experts in the technique of flattening gold into extremely thin sheets. These sheets were used on decorative shields, axes and ceremonial tools such as elaborate knives, idols and masks used in a wide range of cult ritual. Sheets of gold were a highly traded commodity in an area where no pack animals were available (with the exception of llamas to the south in Peru) and all cargo needed to be moved on foot. It was typical to ship in thin sheets of gold from outside the Tarasco region and hire local Aztec artisans for the fine finished work.

Sound, color and vibration were central to virtually all Aztec cult activity and continue to be principle features in contemporary Mexican occult practices. They developed complex rituals utilizing gold and silver but also ceramic and wooden flutes. Bells were uniformly used but they were often accompanied by vocal signals and death whistles which emit a sound like the screams of the dying. Summoning Aztec spirits is no easy task. Almost all rituals require specific songs to be played on properly ensouled instruments. This reverence for the magick of music and the finely tuned effectiveness of sacred sound led the Aztecs to upgrade their ritual instruments whenever possible. They began to adopt gold into their cult material for one major reason: gold makes superior noises to silver or other workable metals. Material archaeological evidence shows that metal alloys were manufactured with specific attributes in mind: sound and color. Copper-tin, copper-arsenic, copper-silver and bronze alloys were employed in amounts sufficient to strengthen the metal object while simultaneously pushing the alloys' colors from reddish toward golden-silvery hues.[1] These hues were prized for their solar correspondences.

The bells made from gold simply sounded richer than the metal alloys the Aztecs were using before information about advanced gold metallurgy made it north to Mexico from Peru. The Aztecs used Andean prototypes of gold ritual tools to engineer their own specialized cult artifacts to fit their own aesthetic and spiritual needs. This insulatory tendency helped maintain the distinct qualities of Aztec ritual technology.

The sound of bells ringing is believed to hold supernatural protective powers connected to the solar association of gold. Descriptive words like tinkling and tingling are used to describe the bells on gods such as Tezcatlipoca.[2] The warrior class had elaborate military costumes of gold bracelets, breastplates, earplugs and bells. The sound of their jangling bells on the knees and wrists provided astral and physical protection to the warriors. Both Tezcatlipoca and Huitzilopochtli are war gods and their devoted warriors were clad in as much gold ornamentation as the idols in the temples.

AZTEC GOLD INTO CATHOLIC CEREMONIAL OBJECTS

When the Spanish arrived in Mexico with their gold-lust they freely robbed the people, hungry for gold even though a sizable cache of wealth was immediately gifted to them. Conquistadors spent their days chasing 'yellow women' to capture and rape, a fetishized obsession flamed by their lust for gold. Given the extensiveness which the Aztecs used gold in their ornamentation and temples, the Spanish came to believe that gold must have been infinite in the area, and that the Aztecs were simply hoarding the rest of their wealth. More likely, the

---

[1] Dorothy Hosler. *Sound, Color and Meaning in Ancient Western Mexico* (World Archeology. Vol 27, no1, June, 1995)
[2] Guilhem Olivier. *Mockeries and Metamorphoses of an Aztec God: Tezcatlipoca, 'Lord of the Smoking Mirror'* (Boulder: University of Colorado Press, 2003)

Aztecs had a starkly different value system, both spiritually and economically, and therefore did not immediately relate to the voraciousness of the Spanish need for gold. If the Spanish had arrived salivating for Jade that may have been a bit more understandable. Rumours that the Spanish ate gold and needed it to survive began circulating.

Regardless of the differences in value between the two cultures, there was nonetheless a near complete transformation of gold Aztec ritual objects into Spanish Catholic ritual objects. The gold was often melted down or otherwise compacted on site in Mexico and shipped back to Europe for re-purposing. A percentage of the gold, gems and other valuables plundered from the Aztecs was to be sent back to the Spanish crown as a return on the investment made on Cortez's voyage. Some gold stayed in Mexico under the usage of the Christian churches.

Just as the Aztec solar temples were razed and built upon to erect Catholic cathedrals, elaborately crafted ritual tools were destroyed and turned into crucifixes and other liturgical objects. Within the Catholic Eucharist ritual, The Most Precious Blood of Christ is always poured into a metal chalice with the interior of the cup lined in gold. Interestingly, in both the Catholic and the Aztec tradition, we see a link between the the sun/son, blood and gold. The essence of indigenous Mexican spirituality literally and ideologically melted into Catholicism during the 17th century, which may explain the ease with which Mexican Catholics also keep shrines to Sante Muerte without contradiction today. Just as gold is a superior conductor metal, it also appears to conduct the predominant solar energy of any given culture.

Bells, so central to Aztec spirit-work, have also been part of the Catholic tradition since the Middle Ages. Spanish Catholic churches were typically smaller local churches rather than grand cathedrals and the large bells were often rung directly by hand instead of by mechanism or rope. Hand bells are rung inside the church during Mass and large church bells mounted to the towers were rung to announce the holy days, deaths of parishioners and to call on worshipers. Bells are used to purify and expel demons as well. The parallels between ancient Mexican and modern Catholic ritual practices transitioned the indigenous Mexica into their colonizer's religion while maintaining a semblance of familiarity.

Unfortunately by the 16th century, entire temples of elaborate Aztec sacred objects were hammered or melted down into easy-to-ship bars once the Spanish retained control over the gold in the region. Although logistically practical, the process devastated a massive amount of Mesoamerican cultural, architectural and religious objects.

Ironically, a portion of stolen sacred gold objects never made it to Spain. During La Noche Triste (Night of Sorrows) on June 30th 1520, Spanish forces massacred 10,000 Aztecs as they celebrated the festival of Tóxcatl. Upon learning of the massacre, Aztec warriors set out for a counter attack. Being outnumbered at the time, the conquistadors in possession of Aztec wealth secretly retreated from their post in Tenochtitlan and ran scattered through the thickly wooded terrain, dropping a significant amount of gold. Some managed to snatch up the smaller precious gems which could more easily be hid on their person. Those who stuffed gold into their pockets were weighed down and apprehended. In the panic of the attack, a significant amount of Spanish and Aztec soldiers drowned in the Mixcoatechialtitlan canal.[3] The remaining gold and valuables were reclaimed by the landscape but this didn't stop Cortez from demanding the gold back from the surrounding tribes.

The remaining gold was documented, packed safely and loaded onto a fleet of merchant ships heading back to Spain. Despite their expensive effort in warring and plundering, English and French pirates waited like vultures for the Spanish fleet just off the Atlantic coast. After the first ship was raided and the artifacts discovered, word spread quickly of the exotic treasures *en route* to Europe. Of course, there is no accounting for the whereabouts of the gold after it was intercepted. However, it is more likely that Mexican gold resides in the UK or the bottom of the Atlantic than Spain.

Gold is the link between cult power, blood energy and the rays of the sun. Instead of Aztec human sacrifices to a solar essence, the Catholic church focuses their energies on one sacrifice; that of the crucified Christ. Although these are much different sacrifices, the alchemical qualities of gold transformed both Mexico and the Spanish Catholic tradition.

SUN AS CENTRAL SPIRITUAL METAPHOR

The Aztec cult was the result of deep traditions of indigenous ancestors tempered in the fire of a bloody golden age. The resulting ethno-religious spiritual practices were intricate, subtle understandings of the spirit world in juxtaposition with a fearless belief in the transformative properties of death. The sun throughout Mesoamerica was a metaphor for the rising and falling of all creatures, especially man. Death was intimately linked to the mystery of the sun and the dependability of both shadowy chaos and radiant light reflected man's experience of himself and the spirit world.

Like man, the daily travel of the sun across the sky is divided: half in the heavens and half in hell. Man is half spirit and half flesh. We rise with the sun as our conscious selves and fall asleep to dream with our subconscious in the dark. Every single night we return to the womb of our spirit-consciousness and bathe in the strangeness that is the great mystery. Every morning, the natural world is awakened and renewed into its logical material reality.

Essentially, the sun itself was a representative of the spiritual and cosmic order of the entire universe. The basic building blocks of time were measured in days, not in minutes or hours. This gives some context as to why the Aztec calendar appears so large and spans several cycles of time. The sun represents time itself in its rotating eternal transformation.

---

3 Miguel León-Portilla. *The Broken Spears The Aztec Account of the Conquest of Mexico* (Boston: Beacon Press, 1962) p.83

EXCREMENT OF THE SUN: HOLY SHIT

The Nahuatl expression for gold is *coztic teocuitlatl*[4], literally 'Yellow Sacred Excrement'. Another variation is *tonatiuh icuitl*[5], 'Excrement of the Sun'. Tonatiuh is the formal name of the Aztec sun god but also refers to the physical sun – the term holy shit applies here but without a trace of the typical contradiction. Similarly silver, which was less favored by the Aztecs, was considered the excrement of the moon. This belief is common in most of Mesoamerica.

In general, the larger veins of gold running through the earth were considered the waste of the sun deposited as it descended into the underworld. The gold which was mined in Western Mexico was imported to Aztec city-states where the elite class of royalty and priests commissioned incredibly elaborate military headgear, breast plates, sun disks and ritual masks. Often, the excrement of the sun was ground down into a fine powder which was much easier to ship. Gold dust along with goldleaf sheets became an available and economically sound ritual material. Gold dust helped to stabilize the Mexican trade economy as well. Quills of easily measured sizes were filled with gold dust and used much like coins. A unique gold standard was established.

Excrement was not viewed as entirely filthy and harmful. It was associated with sexual deviancy and sodomy, which was illegal. Shit was also considered infantile and therefore dangerous to a warrior, which is exactly why some of the Aztec's enemies deterred them by throwing feces at them.[6] But the power shit holds in the form of vice had another side. If something was blasphemous or harmful, it could also heal. In fact, the excrement of the sun was often given medicinally for treatment of pustules, hemorrhoids and warts. Due to its association with sodomy and vice, gold was also prescribed for the prevention of sexually transmitted diseases. Gold dust was taken orally like a pill. If no gold dust was available, small shavings or filings were ingested.

This neutral, if unbalanced view of excrement is further exhibited in Aztec gods and goddesses associated with filth, phlegm, shit, puss and bile. Tlazōlteōtl, for example, is a goddess who eats dirt, filth and shit thereby absolving man of his sin. Her offerings often included urine and feces. Out of these vile substances, however, comes the fertilizer of sacred maize. The god of maize, Cinteotl, *is* Tlazōlteōtl's son. Even waste had a beneficial place in the Aztec material realm and therefore the astral. Tezcatlipoca, the primal god of black magick and night, is often pictured with yellow or gold bands across his face. Equally feared and revered, Tezcatlipoca in the form of Titlacauan was known as 'wretched sodomite'. For a god of the night, Tezcatlipoca was adorned with an exceptional amount of gold in his temples.

Used for both tax tributes to the Aztecs and ritual bodily decorations, gold dust was measured in gourd bowls, enough to fill two cupped hands. The Codex Mendoza lists 20 gourd bowls as an annual amount of money paid to the Aztecs in

---

4 Sahagun, Florentine Codex, 11:233.
5 Sahagun, Florentine Codex, 11:233.
6 Cecelia F. Kline. *Teocuitlatl, 'Divine Excrement': The Significance of 'Holy Shit' in Ancient Mexico* (Art Journal, vol. 52, no. 3, 1993) p26.

the form of gold dust. Cult activities which required gold dust were multitudinous. The fine powder was used to coat the large stone idols or the priests. Several gods are recognizable by distinctive gold bands across their faces, resulting in expensive statues and idols.

Although the excrement of the sun was sacred, socially the hoarding of wealth in the form of gold or other riches was broadly frowned upon. Power and wealth was intended solely for the spirits and royal leadership. It would have been social suicide for anyone but the king to exhibit over-the-top financial resources. Even the elite merchant class was strictly regulated. Hence, excrement is considered dishonest and 'a deadly thing'. Common men who achieved significant wealth which rivaled royalty were 'filthy deceivers'.[7] Greed for gold went well beyond the Aztec moral code which favored balance and self-control.

THE FIFTH SUN

The Aztec ritual cult is largely regarded as one of the most violent and visually decadent indigenous religions in the Western world. Dark as it may appear to outsiders, a vibrant solar cult existed within its complex religious practices. Deeper inquiry into Aztec magical tradition reveals an entirely unique understanding of the word "Sun". While this auspicious title sounds similar to agrarian solar cults throughout the world, the Aztecs were not implying a mere reverence for their celestial heat source, but rather used the word "Sun" to refer to the very seat of power which rules our eon. It was acknowledged by the ancient and classical Aztec peoples that the role of sun god had been filled by several deities in previous eras.

Aztec suns, or eras, were birthed through violence; gradually the sun rose in power and was then destroyed along with all life it supported. Once the cycle was complete, rulership was passed on to the next god. Our time-place is the fifth incarnation, the sun of movement. This movement and the process of life as we know it is fully dependent on blood sacrifice: sacrifice of the gods to create the cosmos and the sacrifice of human hearts to sustain its movement. The fifth sun is not meant to last forever, though. Like all previous epochs, the time will come when all life and matter will catastrophically sink back into the dark primordial form. Whether or not another sun will rise or another humanity created is entirely at the discretion of the primordial gods who remain in the dark. The Aztecs were not exactly hopeful, as they considered the Fifth Sun to be the last one allowed to exist. Their frame of mind was a curious blend of apocalyptic mystical dread and a surprising absence of nihilism usually associated with the former preoccupation. This may not be too far-fetched: astronomers are aware that the star in the center of our planetary system will explode and die out eventually but this does not deter the ongoing pursuit of science and progress in the meantime.

Using a circular timekeeping method which greatly informed their ritual cult calendar, Aztecs calculated the existence of four previous suns. Each sun is referred to by a date-sign which corresponds with the last day that sun existed, which was

---

7 Sahagun, Florentine Codex, 11:234.

also the method of that eon's apocalyptic destruction. Each previous era was ruled by a primordial deity who created and eventually destroyed the world, passing the torch of existence onto the next deity to create or destroy as they wished. The first sun was ruled by the darkest deity in the entire pantheon, Tezcatlipoca, a rather Saturnine spirit of the night and black magick. This sun was the black sun, the dangerous 4 Jaguar.[8] As one might guess, the giant humanoids living during this sun were all mauled and devoured by Tezcatlipoca himself in his fierce jaguar form. Tezcatlipoca then turned the reigns over to his enemy-twin Quetzalcoatl, the feathered serpent who rules the air. Quetzalcoatl's era was 4 Wind,[9] and although the Sun was no longer under the reign of a dark god, the humanoids of the era were blown violently into the trees, became monkeys and were then destroyed. Next came 4 Rain[10], where the god Tloloc was sovereign for a time. Usually benevolent toward humans while bringing essential rain to crops, Tlaloc is also the god of lightning. Sun 4 Rain came to an end when all life was smothered by a rain of fire and lightening from the sky. The proceeding sun, 4 Water[11] was ruled by a goddess, Chalchiuhtlicue. Eventually, all life was drowned in the swirling waters and again the torch had to be passed on. Interestingly, the time-line of this era seems to coincide with deluge myths from other cultures. According to Aztec myth, there were no survivors of this worldwide catastrophe.

Finally we come to our era, the Fifth Sun whose name is Four Movement,[12] the sun of sacred movement, of processes and transformations. Although the sun rose high in the sky on the first day of this eon, it simply shone in a static position, an endless day burning everything in sight. Nothing could grow or exist in this world. In order to establish movement, orbits, seasons and the transformation of life into death, this sun demanded to be fed on the blood of sacrifice. The primordial gods sacrificed themselves in a suicidal jump into the flames to release their energy into the world and set off the proper movements which govern the sky and the growing seasons. As the sun began to rise and set, life and death began their dance. This is quite a collaborative ritual effort on behalf of all the primordial gods. Afterwards, some gods ascended to the heavens and others took their place below the earth, some patrons of life and some of death but all in their proper place. However, this system needed to be maintained, and as the gods had already sacrificed themselves, this left the sacred task to humanity. Theologically speaking, this is the basis for the elaborate ritual of human sacrifice in Mesoamerica. If the Sun received no more energy, no more hearts and no more blood, there would be an eventual degradation of the world which marked the apocalypse. It is already known, as is implied in the very name Four Movement, that our era will collapse from the cataclysmic movements of the earth commonly known as earthquakes. As our era is thought to

---

8 *Naui Ocelotl*. While jaguars are a symbol of Tezcatlipoca because they are apex night predators, ocelots are slightly smaller wild predatory cats native to the Valley of Mexico. Nahuatl to English / Spanish translations often include both as the Nahuatl glyph for the word is the head of a non-distinct spotted feline. See Nicholas J. Saunders. *Icons of Power: Feline Symbolism in the Americas* (London: Routledge, 1998)
9 *Naui Ehecatl*
10 *Naui Quiauitl*
11 *Naui Atl*
12 *Naui Ollin*

be the very last sun, the divine duty of human sacrifice takes on sincere immediacy and dire necessity. There will not be another chance. This is the honor and the duty of the Aztecs. Absolute faith in this theory structurally supported and spiritually justified the ravenousness of the Aztec empire both inwards as well as outwards to the surrounding tribal states.

SOLAR METAPHYSICS

Solar cults were extremely common in ancient agrarian cultures. While the Aztecs did indeed have a 'sun god', the perplexing carousel of interchanging solar attributes from one god to another is unique to Mesoamerica. The Aztec organization of spirits doesn't define them as separate; they bleed readily into each other. Rigid classical organization of iconography or hierarchy was not necessary, as the images of the gods were only used as a ritual interface despite the Aztec reputation for idolatry. Gods were closer to sacred masks than idols.

Truly understanding the nature of the Aztec solar cult is exceedingly difficult for outsiders; in fact it is murky even for Mexicans of Aztec descent. After the conquest of Mexico, people were quite willing to drop the complicated mythology of certain gods which they feared more than loved. This included the national sun god, Huitzilopochtli. For such an important deity, very little is studied about him and there are almost no surviving archaeological materials which give concrete evidence of his cult.

The habit of breaking down the gods into equal compartmentalized offices is a rather European tendency and the addition of Catholicism to the indigenous Mexica religion slanted views of the Aztec gods. Although there are vague associations between classical Greco-Roman gods and the Aztec deities, it was a miscalculation on the part of the Spanish to assume any real correspondences when it came to the function of the spirits themselves. For example, despite being a solar god, Huitzilopochtli was also a patron of warriors and bloodletting so his immediate association was with the classical Mars. The crux of the divide between Aztec and European religious thought is the fluidity of the Aztec pantheon. Deities had both distinctive and collective religious regalia and powers. The wider Mesoamerican belief systems were exercises in a well-ordered and well-centered cosmos, despite this ambiguous fluidity. Divinity itself rests in its powerful vagueness.

For Europeans (and monotheists in general) there instinctually must be one central, elevated god worthy of worship and a plethora of lesser spirits, usually evil. This is a useless lens by which to view the cult of the Aztecs; it confuses the matter even further. For the Aztecs and surrounding Mesoamerican cultures, holiness or sacredness was not a static concept. Every thing and every god continually changes. The sun itself is not sacred – the movement of the sun and therefore the movement of growth it invokes within the earth is sacred. Fluid movements from one identity to another by means of attribute exchange was the norm for Aztec spirits. This causes some confusion in the study of the iconographic or archaeological details of Aztec idols. Hesitant to even use the word deities, it is more accurate to describe the gods as ritual masks, functions or processes. All energy was the self generative *teotl*, the one true force stemming from the primordial dark.[13] All else, the material and astral alike, are but transitory expressions of *teotl*. Underlining the concepts of divinity, the Aztecs categorized all objects, people, places, animals, as either *neltiliztli* or not so much. The closest translation of *neltiliztli* from Nahual to English is truth, although it is clearly applied on sliding scale.[14] This scale is not hierarchical but 'well-centered' or rooted in *teotl*. Some profoundly holy things, like gold, the Templo Mayor, jade, quetzal feathers[15] and properly sanctified and sacrificed human hearts are considered precious and therefore *neltiliztli*. The concealment or un-concealement of *teotl* within a vessel determined its truthfulness.

While other, fouler things like vomit, feces, phlegm and filth were not in the same holy realm, they did indeed have their role in the cosmos. The goddess of shit and semen is just as necessary in the process of fertility as the sun god himself. The holy and unholy needed each other, and neither were barred from the realm of the supernatural. This concept clearly clashes with the invading Spanish Christianity of the 16th century, whose codices are commonly referenced in scholarly pursuits of Aztec metaphysics and religion. Gods and the material world are all fluid and if something exists in our world, it is because *teotl* exists within it. From this perspective there can be no devils. Or, rather, there were many devils and they were in no way disrespected, shunned or considered evil. Understanding the implications of this seemingly contradictory core belief will also reveals the Aztec's uniquely well-centered incarnation of traditional Mesoamerican metaphysics.

SOLAR ASTRAL HOUSES AND ASTROLOGICAL ASPECTS

The Aztec approach to devotion involves ritual interaction with divine masks which leads to extensive astral associations between deities. The sun itself is broken up into separate degrees of transformation, highlighting the heroic journey of the physical sun from bright dawn to the dark underworld. Like gold, the sun is a symbol of alchemical transmutation. The deified sun took on many masks. In stances of power and crisis, it moved through all of its astral houses.

Mystically speaking, Aztecs envisioned the sun as oriented off in the distance where drums and pipes play exuberantly into the air over the eastern waters. The jubilant sun emerges from the womb of a new dawn. The east is representative of rejuvenation and rebirth. This is the same astral realm where warriors, sacrificed men, and women who died in childbirth reside after they die. It is an honor reserved for the bold and fearless in the face of death. They achieve ascension in its highest

---

13 For a discussion of *teotl* and Aztec metaphysics, see James Maffe., *Aztec Philosophy: Understanding a World in Motion* (Boulder: University Press of Colorado, 2014)

14 Maffey, *Aztec Philosophy*, section 2.3

15 Resplendent Quetzal (*Pharomachrus mocinno*) and Eared Quetzal (*Euptilotis neoxenus*) are birds native to western Mexico and Guatemala. Mesoamericans prized their vibrant, iridescent feathers – particularly the long green-gold and blue tail plumage of the males. Despite their fantastic feathers, they are solitary and difficult to locate.

form every day; as long as the sun rises they rise alongside. These souls escort the sun from its first rays, when he wages war on his enemy the Morning Star. At this point the sun is known as Xippilli, The Jeweled Prince, joyous and fresh as he presides over the lush morning splendor of the world.

But the sun's physical and mystical journey did not end there. By midday, the sun became Cuauhtemoc, He Who Swoops Like An Eagle. Considerably fatigued by the close of day, he changes his guise into Tlalchitonatiuh, Earthbound Sun, and begins to set in the western sky. Now his enemy, having changed guise to the Evening Star, emerges to capture and sacrifice the sun. When all of the sun's rays are devoured by the Earth Monster, whose mouth is a gateway to the underworld, the sun becomes completely defeated in his celestial battle. Entering the underworld, the sun is now dead. He is Yohualtonatiuh, the Night Sun. While offering his dark, gloomy rays of weird light to the dead souls in the underworld, the Night Sun becomes withered and foul. Where he was once a fresh Jeweled Prince, he is now a blind, rotting, deformed monster struggling towards his escape.[16] When the night is over, the sun finds his radical transformation and emerges once more over the eastern waters, completely rejuvenated. The entire process begins anew.

As this journey illustrates, the solar astrological houses are expressed in terms of a celestial battlefield. This shows a link between the sun, a religious warrior cult and blood sacrifice in Aztec religion.

The offices of solar energy were occupied by a traditional deity known as Tonatiuh[17] at one point in the Aztec cult. His face, or rather glyph, is well known as the center of the sun calendar. His descriptive titles include He Who Goes Forth Shining, Resplendent One, Heavenly Marksmen[18] and The Eagle, who ascends the sky on fresh morning winds and swoops downwards just like the sun sets. Creation myths tell us of the ultimate transformation of a god named Nanahuatl into the sun. Nanahuatl was a hideous god whose skin was plagued with pustules and ulcers, running open sores and wounds: a divine deformity. His decrepit exterior hid a bold and courageous spirit, as he was the only god who jumped without hesitation into the raging sacrificial fire, initiating creation. This willingness to die for the creation of the cosmos was rewarded when he became the one and only sun. From then on, Nanahuatl was known as Tonatiuh, and demanded the rest of the gods sacrifice themselves as well so that he would have enough blood-energy to rise and set. While Tonatiuh fed on the *teotl* energy inside human hearts and continually practiced auto-sacrifice daily, his astral office morphed slowly into that of Huitzilopochtli. The role became a reflection of the Aztec state itself. It appears that whichever manifestation or mask is being fed and worshiped collects the most *teotl* and therefore becomes the closest to mankind and the easiest to intervene in the material world.

Diligent Aztec astronomers noted that Venus confronted the Sun in battle twice a day. As the Morning Star, divinized as Tlahuicalpantecuhtli, Venus waits

---

16 Roberta H. and Peter T. Markman. *Masks of the Spirit: Image and Metaphor in Mesoamerica* (LA, University of California Press, 1989) Chapter 5: The Temporal Order.
17 Elizabeth H. Boone. *Incarnations of the Aztec Supernatural: The Image of Huitzilopochtli in Mexico and Europe.* (Transactions of the American Philosophical Society, Vol. 79, No.2, 1979) p2.
18 Darts and arrows held solar correspondences due to their similarities with the rays of the sun which pierce the sky.

for the sun to be born with weapon already drawn. As the Evening Star, divinized as Xolotl, Venus gets a second chance to do battle, this time victoriously sacrificing the sun. This celestial mythology is underlined by the fact that the sun and stars are known to be cosmically at odds with each other. Completely opposing forces, the sun represented warmth, light and life whereas the stars were chaotic entities of violent emptiness. All the stars who are opponents of the sun-as-Huitzilopochtli are collectively known as The Four Hundred Huitznahua. Stars in general were perceived as cold and distant in their attempts to wipe out the sun, although this does not deter the Aztec fascination with them. Venus perfectly represents all stars, therefore becoming elevated and concentrated in its evil, but only in its relation to the supreme sun. The sun is always the center of reality.

Aztecs took their highly developed astrological observations very seriously. The Morning and Evening Star, Venus in its two aspects, are especially malignant. In some myths, Venus is the younger brother of the sun. In a reversal of their reverence for the nurturing rays of the sun, rays of the light of Venus are dangerous when in an ill conjunction. The day on which Venus re-emerged after a period of invisibility determined who would be cursed by the evil light of the star. On certain day-signs this meant children were affected, another day-sign indicated women. Regardless, all Venus omens were chaotic. People stayed indoors and away from windows to avoid the evil radiance during this time.

HUITZILOPOCHTLI, DIVINE SOLAR WARLORD

In the effort to expunge all indigenous thought-forms and establish Christianity in the New World, the Spanish friars were quick to point the finger at a number of prominent Aztec deities and dub them devils, evil spirits, imps, and even Lucifer himself. Analogies of classical and diabolical correspondences were equally as common. When confronted with the Templo Mayor in person, which features a duel temple to Huitzilopochtli and Tlaloc, the Spanish struggled to conceive of one deity more vicious than the other. It appeared to them every single Aztec god, even their sun god, had the propensity for the demonic, an assumption that is not far from the truth.

Although solar cults are usually associated with fertility, abundance, patriarchal power and radiance, by the 15th century the Aztec sun god was equal parts blood-drinking and war-centric. Placing Huitzilopochtli in the role of solar god was a gradual process. Other entities once resided in the astral house of the sun, although it is unclear if the transition was induced by the power of the cult or was an exchange of attributes shared amongst deities. Believing in the nature of divisions between solar energy and chthonic energy for example, shows a latent Europeanized frame of mind. For the Aztecs, the concept of such a division went unacknowledged and unaddressed by the priesthood. The common people may have lacked intricate knowledge of the deeper mysteries of the cult, but they were acutely aware of the practices and participated as a whole. As the Aztec empire expanded in territory it also expanded its priesthood which led to an increase in theatrical public rituals.

The principle Aztec solar deity or energy was Huitzilopochtli, conveniently for the Aztecs (and extremely inconvenient for their enemies) also the patron war deity of their expanding empire. In fact, Huitzilopochtli himself represented Mexica expansion and domination. Pre-conquest political variables left an indelible mark on the mystical-theatrical cult of the sun. An incredible amount of effort went into ensuring that the cultural direction of the Aztecs was mirrored perfectly in the supernatural realm. This effort generated odd coincidences and bizarre omens throughout the reign of the Aztecs like a case of empire-wide synchronicity. The rise of the Huitzilopochtli-endorsed Aztec state become favored and protected through their ritual interaction and hefty blood offerings to the sun.

When the Aztecs conquered surrounding areas, their rival patron deity was often replaced with Huitzilopochtli but they did not destroy idols or temples to other deities. It was more useful, energetically speaking, to absorb any fringe or defeated deities and reroute the system of religious and military offerings towards the benefit of the Aztec state. Additionally, the Aztecs simply lacked the citizenry to inhabit and actively control the outposts which they conquered. Rival patron idols were often captured by warriors as the idol represented the martial-spiritual focus of each city-state. Like a game of capture the flag, automatic defeat was assured if the idol was stolen. The connection between patron idols and the military was so strong, the temples doubled as armories. Eventually, this birthed a fierce, bitter resentment towards the Aztecs who seemed to compulsively attack their neighbors. Many city-states gladly sided with the Spanish in overthrowing the Aztec capital.

After being conquered, tributes in the form of eligible warrior sacrifices, gold, crops,[19] or jade were made by the defeated tribe to the Aztec government through the office-temple of Huitzilopochtli. These tributes were equally political and spiritual. The Aztec sun was rising and the solar cult expanding as an ideological symbol for the both ancient and contemporary Mexica.

In an effort to strengthen their national deity, the Aztecs smartly added Huitzilopochtli to a class of feared, demonic spirits. Usually associated with the stars, the enemies of the sun, the *tzitzimime* were an all-female group of sky dwelling demons heavily associated with blood and human sacrifice. Their role was simultaneously to hold up the pillars of the cosmos and on occasion drop them, soaring down to earth in an apocalyptic blood-lust which spared no man. These star demonesses wear red skirts, a powerful symbol of authority. Huitzilopochtli was extended this authority visually by means of a more masculine cape. In combining the solar Huitzilopochtli with the nocturnal *tzitzimime* in iconography, the Aztecs retroactively applied an extremely aggressive disposition fitting of a war deity. It is interesting to note that in the effort to cover all powerful bases, the Aztecs gave their national god both solar and chaotic qualities.

Guided by a spirit, the small ethno-cultural Mexica tribe left their mystical homeland of Aztlan in search of their destiny and empire. In an alternative version, they are guided by an invisible voice. Through the shamanic process of divination and spirit communication, this spirit began as a minor hunting deity but gained an increasingly crucial role in the migration of the tribe. Simply put, the voice of

---

19 Traditionally, Maize is considered the primary offering crop but evidence shows that beans, golden amaranth seeds, and squash were all accepted as tributes. See *Codex Mendoza*.

The final, widest opening of the veil between the human and divine worlds was of course, extraction of a human heart while it still beats. To ensure the heart was intact, this needed to be performed on a conscious living human. A team of four to five priests held the sacrificial party down over a stone altar and used surgical precision to slice through the skin with a razor-sharp flint or obsidian knife. Evidence shows some Aztec obsidian ritual tools cut cleaner than modern surgical scalpels. Then, a heavier stone tool was used by the priest-surgeon to break the sternum without damaging the heart. The beating heart, which exhibited the *ollin* movement and contained the energy-rich *teyolia*, was held high towards the sun. Once the *teyolia* was liberated from the human heart, it transformed once more into a fragment of the sun's heat known as *istli*. Steam from the warm, wet heart could clearly be seen rising upwards which was evidence of the *istli* leaving the heart and reuniting with the sun. Folio 70 of Codex Magliabechiano shows this process and the literal flying of the heart skyward leaving a distinct blood trail. The solar vortex is the force which allows the heart to ascend.

Tools utilized in the process of ritual heart extraction were linked to solar symbolism. The distinctive arched stone altar upon which the sacrificial victim was splayed often bore the glyph of the Fifth Sun, ensuring the sacrifice was properly directed. After the surgical extraction of the heart and the ceremonial lifting of the heart into the air, the organ was placed into a massive stone receptacle known as the *cuauhxicalli*, the Eagle Vessel. Although not every Eagle Vessel was literally in the shape of an eagle, the *cuauhxicalli* atop the Templo Mayor was indeed in the shape a fierce eagle.

BIBLIOGRAPHY

Baquedano, Elizabeth, editor. "Tezcatlipoca as a Warrior: Wealth and Bells." *Tezcatlipoca: Trickster and Supreme Deity*, University Press of Colorado, 2014, pp. 113–134. JSTOR, www.jstor.org/stable/j.ctt128807j.10.

Brundage, Burr Cartwright. *The Fifth Sun: Aztec Gods*, Aztec World. University of Texas Press, Austin. 1979.

Carrasco, David. *City of Sacrifice: The Aztec Empire and the Role of Violence in Civilization*. Beacon Press, Boston. 1999.

Gulson, E. R. Eared Quetzal (Euptilotis neoxenus), version 1.0. In *Neotropical Birds Online* (T. S. Schulenberg, Editor). Cornell Lab of Ornithology, Ithaca, NY, 2013. https://doi.org/10.2173/nb.earque.01.

Hosler, Dorothy. "Sound, Color and Meaning in the Metallurgy of Ancient West Mexico." *World Archaeology*, vol. 27, no. 1, 1995, pp. 100–115. JSTOR, www.jstor.org/stable/124780.

Hosler, Dorothy. "Sound, Color and Meaning in Ancient Western Mexico." *World Archeology*. Vol 27, no1. June 1995.

Kerkhove, Ray. "Dark Religion? Aztec Perspectives on Human Sacrifice." The Dark Side: Proceedings of the Seventh Australian and International Religion, Literature and the Arts Conference, 2002.

warrior makes a suitable sacrifice. This may be why decapitation was a popular alternative to the heart extraction method. After the head is detached, the *tonalli*, pictured in many reliefs as a tangle of snakes exploding from the neck, untwisted themselves as they were set free. Many of these reliefs are depicting the ancient Mesoamerican ball game where the defeated party was traditionally decapitated, their *tonalli* in full view. Skull racks came into use in the temples to exhibit the amount of *tonalli* extracted for the sun. Unlike *teyolia*, the *tonalli* could become separated from the body while still alive, akin to the astral body. Lastly, we have *ihíyotl* which can be compared to sacred breath and emotional desires. It is also the seat of the individual's charisma and ability to influence others with the power of their speech. The liver is the traditional physiological dwelling of *ihíyotl*. Together, these three essences make up the life force which humans are borrowing while alive but must give back to the sun upon death. Surgery was performed on the physical and spiritual body to extract these invisible essences.

Tonalli, which is closely associated with the sun, is the preferred element to energize the sun because it is thought to have been separated from the sun and granted temporarily to humanity in a continuous cycle of life. For this reason, human heart extraction was a primary ritual focus for the Aztecs. *Ollin*, which is the sacred two part back-and-forth movement upon which the cosmos is based, is evident in the heartbeat. By freeing this movement that governs the *tonalli*, humans take their dutiful place in sustaining the eon of the Fifth Sun. This process transforms a ritual death into renewed life; it is the necessary recycling of energy.

Solar portals could be opened in a number of ways. Upon the occasion of the New Fire Ceremony, a 52 year cycle of the sun was coming to a close. This auspicious occasion called for the extraction and burning of human hearts to prevent the apocalyptic end of the Fifth Sun. In burning the hearts, the priests released both the *tonalli* as well as the *teyolia*. As the fire engulfed the hearts, the smoke and steam wafted up to feed the sun. This sacred fire opens the necessary portal to allow for solar feeding of hearts and blood.

Another, more common method of portal opening focuses on the use of *ollin* movement within the blood. Before the formal ritual of heart extraction, the priests (and sometimes pious commoners) pierced themselves with maguey spines in the appropriate areas to spill blood. Strings or twine were laced through the wounds to enhance blood-flow. It was thought that this excessive auto-sacrifice was enough to create spiritual openings or 'cracks between the worlds'[26] and so was done liberally leading up to the ritual sacrifice. This bloodletting also called the solar god down to earth, which was no easy feat. In their religious songs and poetry, the Aztecs describe how silent, inexorable and downright stony their gods' dispositions often were.[27] They were not going to show up at all unless they were assured it was worth their time. Even then, it was wise to have plenty of food and drink ready for them upon arrival.

---

26 Irene Nicholson. *Firefly in the Night: A Study of Ancient Nahuatl Poetry and Symbolism* (New York: Grove Press, 1959) p44.
27 Ray Kerkhove. *Dark Religion? Aztec Perspectives on Human Sacrifice. The Dark Side* (Proceedings of the Seventh Australian and International Religion, Literature and the Arts Conference, 2002) p147.

Astrally speaking, the entire ritual operation of human sacrifice directed towards the sun emulated the Aztec ideal of spiritual ascent. There was no higher spiritual office than the solar office and in order to ascend, one must die accordingly. For this reason alone, all sacrifices must be entirely voluntary. Working solar magic was the sole responsibility of the various priesthoods, but common people were willing and eager participants in the cult. The ritual space in which the majority of the solar magic was performed, the Templo Mayor, was the place in which political, economic and mystical realms met at a single point. This point is the axis of the cosmos, where the sun and all the gods were birthed: the navel of the world. Quite literally, the Templo Mayor and Tenochtitlan as a whole were the only places where heaven, earth and the underworld met on the same plane. It was here that the Aztecs could properly perform ceremonies and sacrifices which opened up the gateway or portal to release and direct the blood-energy to the sun.

SPIRITUAL SURGERY: ASTRAL MECHANICS OF HUMAN HEART EXTRACTION

The most integral aspect of solar magic is the highly technical and ritualized process of human heart offerings. The side-effect of this offering was, of course, a human death. As the Aztecs largely suspected life to be only a hallucination, that side-effect was not particularly outrageous. Warriors between the ages of 20 and 30 were the most likely to have their hearts offered up, but about a fifth of those sacrificed by this method were women and even a small portion of children.[25] Statistics like these confirm the assertion that locals were sold into slavery as a means to supply Tenochtitlan with blood to feed the sun.

Regardless of which entity wore the solar mask during the ritual, there are consistencies across the board in terms of the technique and ritual tools. The energy was directed towards the office of the sun, and yet this ritual could be successfully performed at a wide range of temples, not all overtly solar.

No ritual could be performed without first opening the proper vortex. To understand how and why this was done, we must examine the three energetic components which comprise all life: *teyolia*, *tonalli* and *ihíyotl*. *Teyolia* is the animating force itself, the vitality of the living world. *Teyolia* is present in mountains, rivers, cities, animals and plants but in the human it is concentrated in the heart. It cannot be separated from the living human. This is where all the person's knowledge and lifeforce stems. It is the only part which stays with the consciousness of the individual even after death because it is immortal. Next we have *tonalli*, closely associated with the heat of fire, particularly the burning of the sun. It is the passion by which humans develop and forge their destiny. It also determines the personality or astrology of an individual upon birth, both considered unalterable. When one begins to age and grow feeble or ill, it is the *tonalli* which is deteriorating. *Tonalli* is thought to reside in the head, which is why the hairlock, skull and scalp of a

---

[25] Lizzie Wade. *Feeding the gods: Hundreds of skulls reveal massive scale of human sacrifice in Aztec capital* (Science Magazine, 2018).

like rotten fruit. Its link to the glowing sun was severed with an obsidian blade but pushed out of sight the way one gobbles a mealy apple so as not to waste it and then longs for a better apple.

It was reported that the Aztec priests often mocked and sarcastically jested the Christians for their shock and distaste for human sacrifice. For the Aztecs it was widely agreed that how one died was much more important than anything done while living, halfway mirroring the Christian ethics and martyrdom. Often, men would demand to be sacrificed as it was the only means to obtain eternal status within the group of spirits which rose with the morning sun. A similar self-sacrifice is found in the Japanese Samurai tradition of Seppuku. Dying bravely, voluntarily and tortuously was the only way out of the underworld and into a brighter realm.

Voluntary sacrifice was often performed to atone for a perceived sin. It was generally understood that any immoral act, *tlatacolli*, was an error that could have widespread and devastating effects on the larger community. To sin in the personal, private life affected the weather, the economy and the overall health of the culture. Both men and women could volunteer as a sort of sacrificial martyr to pay for the collective misdeed even if the exact sin could not be identified. Once the sun was fed an extra meal, the People of the Sun could return to a relative normal.

SITES OF RITUAL SOLAR MAGIC

Much of the information we have available regarding the details of the Aztec solar cult is built upon material archaeology. This includes the temples themselves, the icons they housed within the temples as well as remnants of the bloody sacrifices performed in the area. Often, the solar temples can be identified by the excessively thick patina from decades of dried blood. The foremost temple used in ritual solar magic was the Templo Mayor. Interestingly, it was already ancient ruins when the Aztecs came upon it. A process of not only re-building but over-building their temples promptly began during the founding of Tenochtitlan. Despite their nostalgic enthusiasm, the Aztecs really had no idea which deities were worshiped in the ruined temples. The original structures were added onto in several stages while remaining in use. The higher the Aztecs rose in their empire, the higher the pyramids rose until they reached steep proportions. Literally, they were bridging the gap between themselves and the sun to which they directed sacrifices. Upon the fall of the Aztec empire, the Templo Mayor was crushed and the outer stones re-purposed toward the building of a rather basic Spanish cathedral. Within a few years, the basic cathedral was given a considerably expensive upgrade and built onto again to form the Mexico City Metropolitan Cathedral. We can see that this site has been built upon repeatedly, effectively re-routing the solar office many times: beginning with mysterious pre-historic Mesoamerican deities for which dirt mound-altars and more permanent stone platforms were built, to the dual Aztec gods Huitzilopochtli-Tlaloc of the grand Templo Mayor to the Churrigueresque cathedral honoring the divinity of the Roman Catholic faith – all in a continual lineage. To say the area is spiritually active is an understatement.

collective, the "People of the Sun". Not only did they assume the social status of the highest solar association, they were also blessed with precious materials associated with the divinity of the sun, namely gold.

When Huitzilopochtli spoke to the shaman-priest Cuauhtlequetzqui in the days of Aztec migration, he described his vision to his people: "There our name will be praised and our Aztec nation made great. The might of our arms will be known and the courage of our brave hearts. With these we shall conquer nations, near and distant, we shall subdue towns and cities from sea to sea. *We shall become lords of gold and silver...* "[23]

The Aztecs did seem blessed in warfare and they inherited significant wealth under sole sponsorship of Huitzilopochtli but that may be expected when such a faithful population shed blood towards one goal. In public ritual and in war, the Aztec empire as a group acted not only on behalf of the gods, but as a unified magical body accurately directing the flow of blood-energy from the human world back into the sun where it rightfully belonged. It doesn't hurt to develop an elite military class so terrifying in battle they had a tendency to announce their presence loudly and assume complete submission from the opposing people. Often, this was indeed enough. If Aztecs were met in battle it was often the sole purpose of the warrior to maim the opposing men, claim their hearts for sacrifice to his sun god and return them to his home temple. There was a common distinction between war meant to conquer and the Flower Wars, meant to maim or draw blood to feed the gods rather than slay an enemy in battle. The warriors caught in these Flower Wars were often close to death when they were made to drink alcoholic *pulque*, then forced to dance into Tenochtitlan where they were dubbed "Children of the Sun" and waited in line to be sacrificed *en masse*.

Some contemporary sources choose to paint the Aztecs as unfairly judged and downplay their mass human sacrifices to the sun, but that sentiment disregards the extensive archaeological evidence and decoded glyphics which confirms a long history of human sacrifice in Mesoamerica. The argument that Spanish sources over-exaggerated may hold some weight theoretically, but the practice of human sacrifice did indeed exist on a large scale regardless of the final head (or skull) count.[24] If the victims were chosen at random, or if the Aztecs preyed on the weak or sick, that would not make a proper sacrifice at all. No one was hunting these individuals in foreign areas, all were residents of, or assimilated into, the city-state of Tenochtitlan. As the People of the Sun, they had a duty to find suitable, high quality candidates from the royal or military class. For certain festivals, 'bathed slaves' could be offered up by the mercantile class in lieu of their own life. It might seem incredible that most people went willingly to the sacrificial stone but that was the norm and the ideal situation for the ritual. If by chance someone being escorted to their death hesitated or showed fear that was a bad omen. A weak sacrifice was

---

23 Miguel Leon-Portilla. *Pre-Columbian Literatures of Mexico* (Norman: University of Oklahoma Press, 1968) p87.
24 Archaeological findings in Mexico City show that parts of the Templo Mayor were constructed by double sided walls of the skulls of sacrificed individuals, 75% of which were men of prime warrior age. NIAH reports that skulls lay in rows of up to 120 ft and consist of skinned human skulls layered in between lime mortar.

Huitzilopochtli guided the Mexica south in search of a sign. Along the way, crude earth altars were constructed and the all-important sacred bundle was temporarily unwrapped. Sacred bundles, *tlaquimilolli*, are of utmost cult importance throughout the matrix of Mesoamerican cult practices. Not only is the fabric of the bundle itself sacred and magically potent, but its contents of sacred objects along with the ceremonial opening of the *tlaquimilolli* all function to protect and maintain an energetic connection to the deity. This bundle is essentially a fully functional mobile altar for a temporarily nomadic people. It was the "container of the power of the cult".[20] We see magical parallels in the ensouled effigies of holy icons and the use of poppets in folk magic.

Trusting the mystical voice of Huitzilopochtli proved to be a wise choice, as the tribe received many omens and directions in their journey.[21] In 1325, in a dank swamp territory quite overlooked by other tribes, the group came through the Valley of Mexico and in the middle of lake Texcoco, they were given a final omen: an eagle, the solar symbol of Huitzilopochtli, perched on a nopal cactus pad growing out of a rock in the center of the lake. In its gnashing beak was a writhing serpent. This symbol continues to be used as the symbol for all of Mexico; its importance cannot be understated.

It should be noted that although the Aztecs as a whole worshiped Huitzilopochtli as their national and patron war-god, the actual priesthood of Huitzilopochtli was limited. There were upwards of 5000 priests in the god's service which was a common enough number for a major god. However, the children which were chosen and molded into the priesthood were only taken from the neighborhoods known to be inhabited by the ethnic Mexica.[22] There were no exceptions to this restriction except when the priesthood overlapped with those of Huitzilopochtli's mother, Tezcatlipoca and the rain god Tlaloc (with whom he shared his dual temple). In this case, children of other ethnic groups were permitted some intimate usage of Huitzilopochtli's idols and temples. Perhaps the Mexica, founders of Tenochtitlan, were a reasonable choice to carry on the priesthood of Huitzilopochtli. After all, the god chose to speak to them directly, indicating some level of being the 'chosen' tribe. There is no evidence of any hostile racial overtones regarding this ethnic limitation, although there were some religious tensions between the Mexica and other tribes in earlier times due to their sudden and aggressive religious practices within the urban areas.

PEOPLE OF THE SUN

The higher the Aztecs rose economically, spiritually and militantly, the higher Huitzilopochtli rose in astral offices and power until finally reaching the pinnacle: solar god. As Huitzilopochtli's people, they began to call themselves as a cultural

---

20 *Codex Mednoza*, p41.
21 See *Codex Boturini* for maps of the Mexica migration.
22 Burr Cartwright Brundage. *The Fifth Sun: Aztec Gods, Aztec World* (Austin: University of Texas Press, 1979) p147.

Leon-Portilla, Miguel. *Pre-Columbian Literatures of Mexico*. University of Oklahoma Press, Norman, 1968.

León-Portilla, Miguel. *The Broken Spears: The Aztec Account of the Conquest of Mexico*. Beacon Press, Boston, 1962.

Markman, Roberta H., and Peter T. Markman. *Masks of the Spirit: Image and Metaphor in Mesoamerica*. Berkeley: University of California Press, 1989.

Nicholson, Irene. *Firefly in the Night: A Study of Ancient Nahuatl Poetry and Symbolism*. Grove Press, New York, 1959.

O'Reilly, Joseph P. "On the Mode of Ringing or Sounding Bells in the Early Churches of Northern Spain and of Ireland." Proceedings of the Royal Irish Academy (1889-1901), vol. 6, 1900, pp. 489–502. JSTOR, www.jstor.org/stable/20488788.

Olivier, Guilhem. *Mockeries and Metamorphoses of an Aztec God: Tezcatlipoca, 'Lord of the Smoking Mirror'*. University of Colorado Press, Boulder. 2003.

Palencia-Roth, Michael. "The Conquistadors: First-person Accounts of the Conquest of Mexico. Edited and translated by Particia de Fuentes. New World Encounters. Edited by Stephen Greenblatt.," *Comparative Civilizations Review*: Vol. 35 : No. 35 , Article 7, 1997. https://scholarsarchive.byu.edu/ccr/vol35/iss35/7.

Roskamp, Hans. "God of Metals: Tlatlauhqui, Tezcatlipoca and the Sacred Sumbolism of Metallurgy in Michoacan, West Mexico. *Ancient Mesoamerica*, vol. 21, no. 1, 2010, pp. 69–78. JSTOR, www.jstor.org/stable/26309088.

Saunders, Nicholas J. *Icons of Power: Feline Symbolism in the Americas*. Routledge, London, 1998.

Saunders, Nicholas J. "Cosmic Earth: Materiality and Mineralogy in the Americas". *Soils Stones and Symbols Cultural Perceptions of the Mineral World*. Ed Nicole Boivin. Ed Mary Ann Owoc. Abingdon: UCL Press. 2004.

Stresser-Pean, Guy. *The Sun God and the Savior: The Christianization of the Nahua and Totonac in the Sierra Norte De Puebla, Mexico*. (Mesoamerican Worlds: From the Olmecs to the Danzantes). Edited by Davíd Carrasco and Eduardo Matos Moctezuma. University Press of Colorado, Boulder. 2009.

Sugiyama, Nawa, et al. "Inside the Sun Pyramid at Teotihuacan, Mexico: 2008–2011 Excavations and Preliminary Results." *Latin American Antiquity*, vol. 24, no. 4, 2013, pp. 403–432. JSTOR, www.jstor.org/stable/23645621.

Wade, Lizzie. "Feeding the Gods: Hundreds of skulls reveal massive scale of human sacrifice in Aztec capital". *Science Magazine*. June, 2018. doi:10.1126/science.aau540.

Treasure of Heart Essence

The revelations of the great yogini Sera Khandro

By Verónica Rivas (Melong Yeshe)

Even without worldly ways, my mind is carefree.
Even having been expelled from the community, I accomplished my purpose.
Even though everyone criticized me, I am victorious over all.
Even though they exiled me to a distant land, my mind is resolved.

Sera Khandro

IN TANTRIC or Esoteric Buddhism, the teachings or elements that lead to the highest achievements constitute doctrinal bodies to which access is conditioned by the development of certain qualities, which are necessary to attain the required understanding of them. These doctrinal bodies, known as *termas*, are true magical treasures which constitute authentic keys that open the doors to higher realizations. They can be methods, explanations or advice that establish a bridge between the ordinary mind and the enlightened one. All this is framed by the tantric conception that we are always the enlightened mind, but because of the confusion of our mind we do not perceive it. In this conception, our daily life and our human body are the most precious sources in attaining the supreme *siddhis* (spiritual realizations).

This text is situated in the tradition of magical treasures known as *termas* as they were developed in Esoteric Buddhism and more precisely within Tibetan Buddhism. I could not write about these treasures without referring to the remarkable woman known as Sera Khandro. Since I started my journey on this spiritual path, focusing specifically on the Vajrayana tradition, I began to see myself overcome by difficulties that appeared in my daily practice. But abandoning my spiritual quest did not seem to be an option no matter how hard I tried. During this time, I started to find biographies of female practitioners that had to face the struggles of being a woman in traditions mainly dominated by men in addition to being wives, mothers or women with "arranged marriages" since their childhood. The story of Sera Khandro as a treasure revealer is not the account of a nun, of woman who renounces the world to devote herself to contemplation, but of somebody who lived a "worldly experience of life" as a mother, a rejected woman, and a misunderstood wife. The story of Sera Khandro represents the certainty that to conquer the highest achievements, the courage and strength to live in the world are more effective means than renunciation.

A *terma* is a treasure. According to the Buddhist perspective it could be a kind of instruction or method which is capable of granting great accomplishment, or a material object with a magical and symbolical meaning.

Tulku Thondup Rinpoche says about Buddhist *termas*:

There have been many occasions in world history when scriptures and material objects have been discovered miraculously through the power of spirits, non-human beings and sometimes through psychic powers possessed by gifted human individuals. *Termas* are a kindred phenomenon. They are scriptures that have been deliberately concealed and discovered at successively appropriate times by realized masters through their enlightened power. *Termas* are teachings representing a most profound, authentic and powerful tantric form of Buddhist training. Hundreds of *Tertons*, the Discoverers of Dharma Treasures, have found thousands of volumes of scripture and sacred objects hidden in earth, water, sky, mountains, rocks and mind. By practicing these teachings, many of their followers have reached the state of full enlightenment, Buddhahood.[1]

A *terma* is a kind of key that when properly used can lead the practitioner to perceive the true nature of his mind, which is enlightenment. A *terma* is not going to turn us into a Buddha[2] but its purpose is to offer us a method

---

1 Thondup Rinpoche, *Tulku. Hidden Teachings of Tibet. An Explanation of the Terma Tradition of Tibetan Buddhism.* Edited by Harold Talbott. (Ed. Wisdom Publications, USA, 1997) 13.

2 In this case, we are not referring to the historical Buddha known as Shakyamuni, but to a state of mind. It means the intrinsic Buddha nature, the real essence of our mind as it is taught in the Vajrayana tradition.

that leads us to recognise our truly Buddha nature, or in other terms, the real essence of our mind. It is believed that the tradition of *terma* as it was developed in tantric Buddhism began with the great yogi and tantric Master Padmasamvabha. As we mentioned before, *Termas* can refer to both material things such as sacred artefacts or scrolls as well as to mind treasures. The last type of treasure we mention are mainly practices focused on certain topics, deities or specific methods. But, who was Padmasamvabha and why did he need to hide *termas*?

There are many stories about Padmasamvabha, and most of them highlight his miraculous origin. For example, the most well-known legend about him tells us that he did not have a conventional birth. It is said that he appeared on a lotus flower and was found by a king who did not have offspring. Apparently, one day, Padmasambhava left his family to live his spiritual path following his own insights. He is associated with the place of Uddiyana or Odiyana, also called Orgyen. This place is also associated with other sages and mystics, such as Tilopa, and its geographical position is subject to speculation among scholars. Some of them locate this place in Swat Valley, now Pakistan, and others in Orissa.

It is said that Padmasamvabha received many of his initiations and great realizations directly from the *ḍākinīs* and in places like inhospitable caverns, cemeteries and cremation places. He was considered a great practitioner, a magician of great accomplishments who learned different methods belonging to different traditions. Many sources point out that he was responsible for the introduction of Buddhism in Tibet. Before the arrival of Padmasambhava, other great teachers went to Tibetan lands carrying Buddhist beliefs but all failed in their task. It is said the reason for this is that Tibet was dominated by strong forces and demonic spirits, who were the deities of the predominant Bon religion.

Padmasamvabha is known by other names such as Guru Shantarakshita, Guru Shankya Senge, Guru Padma Jugne, Guru Dorje Totreng, Vajra Guru, among others. It is said that he subjugated negative forces and that his power could banish opposing spirits. Through his practices he demonstrated great mastery of the vehicle of the Sutra and the vehicle of the Mantra,[3] reaching the highest tantric realizations. For all this Padmasambhava is considered the great tamer of *maras*.[4] His power to subjugate spirits and beings did not depend on the favour of gods or spirits but on the very essence of his mind. If we consider this yogi outside the Buddhist doctrines, we can conclude without doubt that he was a great mystic and magician who achieved high realizations and was a great adept of the tantric path.

> Over time, Padmasambhava came to be known by many names and in the guise of numerous manifestations. The surviving representations in literature and art reflect only a fraction of the multiple

---

[3] The Vehicle of the Sutra refers to the religious discourses attributed to a Buddha, and the Vehicle of the Mantra (also known as the Path of the Tantra) refers to esoteric rituals and meditation practices used as tools to attain enlightenment.

[4] *Mara* can be considered as anything that could obstruct the path to enlightenment.

traditions and practices existing at one time or another. Yet mythological themes common from the earliest to the latest sources on Padmasambhava include his role in pacifying and converting local worldly deities, especially in the Himalayas; his status as a cultural hero of tantric ritual; and his preference for highly advanced forms of Esoteric Buddhism. The biographical and iconographical traditions on Padmasambhava create not just another saint, but the founder of a religious lineage and embodiment of tantric Tibetan Buddhism akin to the Buddha and founders of other world religions.[5]

Padmasambhava seems to have spread out tantric Buddhist teachings in Tibet during the time of Emperor Trisong Detsen, approximately in the 8th century CE. The importance of Guru Rinpoche (another way of referring to Padmasambhava) was intensified among the Nyigma tradition, which claims to have an uninterrupted lineage since the time of Padmasambhava. This school has a very rich *terma* tradition. There are among its teachings large volumes dedicated to *terma* revelations and commentaries about them that were progressively discovered by *tertons* throughout time. *Tertons* are those practitioners who have accumulated the necessary merit to be discoverers or developers of great treasures which can lead beings to ultimate realization. Among the Nyigma tradition, it is said that *tertons* are the reincarnations of direct disciples of Padmasambhava or emanations of Yeshe Tsogyal,[6] who attained great accomplishments.

According to the tradition of *terma* it is said that there were teachings that if revealed in the wrong time or to the wrong people would not bring benefit to anyone. Padmasambhava maintained that the teachings should be adapted to the different times and hindrances that beings went through, so that they could take advantage of them. Certain practices or knowledge must be hidden until the proper time. In relation to this, there is a story that tells that Yeshe Tsogyal, concerned with the imminent departure of her teacher, prepared a great offering and asked Padmasambhava to, out of compassion, reveal a practice suitable for times when people would not have the auspicious conditions to devote themselves to a spiritual path, to the search for truth. Then, from the enlightened mind of her teacher emanated one of the most precious treasures: the practice of Red Tara.[7] This was implanted in the mind of one of the disciples present there and would then flourish some centuries later.

---

5 Doney, Lewis. "Padmasambhava in the Conjured Past". *Second Buddha: Master of Time*, Tang Teaching Museum and Rubin Museum of Art, 2018, pp.54-84.

6 *Yeshe Tsogyal*: her name means "Victorious Ocean of Primordial Wisdom". She was a Tibetan woman who attained enlightenment and was considered a great guru in her own right. It is said that Padmasambhava asked her to hide *termas* for the benefit of future generations. She is considered a deity.

7 The story says that approximately 1000 years after Padmasambhava's revelation, the treasure of the practice of Red Tara was codified by a great Nyigma Lama known as Apong Terton. Its formal name is "The Condensed Essence of the Treasure of the Supreme Enlightened Mind: The Mandala Ritual of the Noble Red Tara Called the Wishfulfilling Essence".

We cannot talk about treasures among the Buddhist tradition without referring to the *ḍākinīs* since they are the guardians of treasures *par excellence*, even though they are not the only kind of beings who guard or protect treasures. Among the *terma*'s literature we can read about those guarded by nagas,[8] or by guardians of the land. In this case, the guardians of the land are spirits who dwell in specific places such as caves, old trees, lakes, etc. They are generally non-human spirits that could be worshiped or honoured as minor deities or as messengers of other fully enlightened beings.

Ḍākinīs have a very important role in tantric or esoteric Buddhism even though their origins date from earlier times. The earliest evidence of the existence of these female spirits can be found in the Indus Valley civilizations. Most scholars believe that they have their origin in tribal or indigenous goddesses that assumed different roles with the progressive changing and development of societies. According to the Vajrayana tradition, *ḍākinīs* (*mkha'-'gro-ma*) are emanations or manifestations of the enlightened activity of meditational deities (*yidam*). It is said that the *ḍākinī* is who really confers enlightenment to the practitioner; without her intervention we would not be able to access the real essence of our mind.

As we already mentioned, the figure of the *ḍākinī* precedes Buddhism; in other traditions they have different attributions to those that will be found later with the introduction of these spirits into the Buddhist doctrine. For example, in Hinduism we find them as assistants or messengers of goddesses like Kali[9] or Chinamasta.[10] Here they present a completely fierce aspect as great destroyers and blood drinkers that fulfil protective and exterminating roles. They are not portrayed as fully enlightened beings. In Japan we find the *Ḍākinīten*, who in some cases is considered a messenger of the god Inari[11] but in other sources she appears as an independent deity. Associated with foxes, she is considered a giver of treasures and power. This is what we find in a story in which a general, already losing a battle, saw in front of him a fox which immediately turned into a beautiful woman. This woman, in exchange for his adoration, granted triumph to the general, as well as material treasures and spiritual realizations such as clairvoyance and great meditative abilities.

The function of the *ḍākinī* in Vajrayana Buddhism is of a guardian of treasures; she is the one who opens the doors of knowledge for a practitioner. It is said that without the *ḍākinī* no realization can be achieved. The different traditions offer us several classifications of these

---

8 Serpentine spirits who guarded treasures and sacred places. In Hinduism, they are related to fertility, abundance but also with wisdom.

9 *Kali* is a Hindu goddess whose first appearance is as destroyer of evil forces. She is the feminine manifestation of time, so she is the embodiment of impermanence and existence itself. Many tantric traditions worshiped her as a Divine Mother, as the source of creation and as a divine protector.

10 *Chinamasta* is a Hindu goddess who represents the life-giver and the life-taker. She is portrayed as a nude young beautiful woman holding her own severed head and feeding with her blood her two assistances (*ḍākinīs*). She is also known in Buddhist literature as *Chinnamunda*.

11 *Inari* is a Japanese god of agriculture and abundance. His emissaries are generally foxes. He can be depicted as a man, as a woman or as an androgynous being.

beings, but in a broader and more general way we can say that they are classified between *worldly ḍākinīs* and *fully enlightened ḍākinīs*.[12] This classification is interpreted in many ways according to the level of practice, but it generally refers to the fact that a *ḍākinī* can manifest in unsuspected ways, in different circumstances and places. All meditative practices are no more than a way of preparing the mind to recognize the *ḍākinī*[13] and understand her language to obtain her empowerments.

Treasures can be classified into two types: *earth treasures* and *pure visions and treasures of intention*. The *earth treasures* are usually scrolls written in a symbolic language, known as the language of the *ḍākinīs*. The purpose of this is so they can only be deciphered by qualified people who hold the necessary realization and qualification to be able to transmit such profound teachings. *The pure vision treasures and treasure of intention* are visionary treasures that come primarily from the mind of the bodhisattvas[14] in the form of precious doctrines and visionary teachings. These treasures are a kind of key that appears in the minds of those who have gathered the necessary merit to reach and understand them, being able to reveal great doctrines that lead to the highest *siddhis*. These treasures appear only to those who have such a strong commitment with the practice that they develop skills that allow them to understand the *terma* and teach it to other beings. According to one of the most notable Vajrayana masters of the 20th century, Dudjom Rinpoche, the first *terton* seems to have been Sangye Lama, a monk who followed the tradition of the mantra.

A very important condition, according to the Vajrayana School, is that the discoverer of the *terma* is somebody who has no doubt about dedicating himself to the search of truth and to the practice of the method that was revealed to him. To be a revealer or discoverer of a *terma* is not something that could be considered as a gift which only produces joy and happiness. It is a commitment, a task that must be carried out and fulfilled. It is the obligation of the discoverer of a *terma* that it reaches the greatest number of beings and benefits them immensely. This is not an easy task and the story of Sera Khandro is proof of this. As we will see later, her life was far from being simplified; instead she was constantly being put in front of difficult situations to test her courage and her commitment.

But, how do we know that a teaching or a group of practices are really a *terma*? Is there any form of validation? This is a complicated issue not only in our time where "gurus" appear everywhere, but also since the tradition of *termas* began. Throughout history many people called *tertons* have failed in proving the genuineness of their revelations. The reason for this is because, supposedly, if these doctrines or teachings do not meet certain requirements, they cannot be considered a valid *terma*. But the problem is that many times, these requirements are nothing more than

---

12 For more information about this topic, see the excellent work of the scholar Judith Simmer-Brown *Dakini's Warm Breath. The Feminine Principle in Tibetan Buddhism*.

13 Among the tantric tradition, a human female practitioner who has attained realizations can also be considered a *ḍākinī*.

14 A being dedicated to the altruistic purpose of remaining in the cyclic existence until all beings are free from suffering.

conventions that often have political interests in the predominance of a lineage.

Within the community of academics and scholars whose research focuses on the history and development of Buddhism, there seems to be a consensus that there is no physical and verifiable evidence that Padmasambhava really hid *termas* in the sense of objects such as artefacts, scrolls or images. We find in Sera Khandro's autobiography stories in which she tells us that through dreams she was revealed places where she later found scrolls. The point is that there is nothing that can really prove that these scrolls were written by Padmasambhava or by Yeshe Tsogyel. But, if they were written by someone else, we could analyse the possibility of considering a *terma* a seed, placed magically by the great tantric master in the minds of practitioners in any times and places, that could function as keys of great teachings, though this would be a controversial topic for many Buddhist lineages.

According to Tantric Buddhism, everything that comes from the enlightened mind is a treasure and is a valid *terma*. But when they speak of validity, they are not referring to the logical and ordinary sense of the term, but to a more transcendental meaning, since *terma* is considered to be a revelation. Here, some teachers, especially of the Nyigma school, point out that a *terma* should be analysed considering its "outer", "inner" and "secret" meanings. This corresponds to the Three Kayas.[15]

---

15 *Three Kayas: nirmanakaya* (the physical manifestation of the Enlightened mind); *dharmakaya* (the essence of the mind as vacuity) and *sambhogakaya* (the pure expression of the Enlightened mind).

In this way, everything that is the product of the enlightened mind is a *terma*, because it is considered a path that, from the point of view of the tantric teachings, establishes a bridge between the ordinary mind and the enlightened one. This would be like saying, if the method works then it is authentic, although this seemingly fragile method of validation does not convince many sceptical minds. There are *termas* that are considered true treasures revealed by some schools, but they are considered "invalid" by others.

Apparently, it would take supernatural abilities to really evaluate the authenticity of a *terma*. It is known that there are different kinds of *terma* in other traditions such as the Hindu, the Bon or in some spiritual paths that flourished and developed in China. It is said that the *Perfection of Discriminative Awareness (Prajnaparamita)* sutras were revealed to Nagarjuna[16] in the form of treasure by a serpentine water spirit (*naga*). It is also believed that there were *sadhanas* (sacred ritualistic texts) of the *Mahayoga Tantras* that were revealed to eight masters in a charnel ground. It is probable that the validation criteria for these different kinds of *termas* are not the same.

The interpretation of *termas* as kind of keys that the great master Padmasambhava hid in the minds of his disciples, as mentioned above, applies perfectly to the visionary processes of Sera Khandro. In her autobiography she describes how she found and discovered parts of treasures through lucid dreams and visions. In a propitious moment, as

---

16 He is considered one of the most important Buddhist philosophers. Some sources point out that he was from South India.

if they were pieces of a puzzle, these parts would compose a deep doctrinal body that would form the basis of her teachings and legacy.

The visionary experiences of Sera Khandro

Sera Khandro was a prominent female practitioner, considered in some lineages as a wise and influential master because of her revelation of very important *termas*. In her we can find the descendant of a noble and political influential family, the beggar, the mother, the devoted practitioner and the *ḍākinī*. But the importance of this great practitioner transcends her being a revealer of treasures – her life is an example of persistence, devotion, and is a source of inspiration for many women.

> I, this inferior woman,
>   will tell you
>   a bit about my
>   circumstances —
>   from the time I was seven,
>   *ḍākinīs* took care of me;
>   they reassured me in reality,
>   in visions, and in dreams.
>   From the time I was eleven,
>   the Master Accomplished
>   Awareness Holder
> Saraha took care of me
>   and bestowed ripening
>   [empowerments] and
>   liberating [instructions]
>   upon me.
>   When I reached the age
>   of twelve, I obtained
>   the genuine prophetic
>   guide of the
> *Ḍākinīs'* Oral Transmission
>   Profound Treasure.
>   From the time I was
> thirteen, I exerted myself
>   only in benefiting others.
>   At fourteen, in accordance
>   with the *ḍākinīs* command,
>   I came eastward to the
>   land of eastern Tibet, which
>   is like the demons' island.
>   Not dying, while living
>   I experienced the
>   suffering of hell.[17]

With these words, Sera Khandro completely defines her path and the struggles she endured almost all of her life. Because of the types of hindrances she had to overcome, many times she felt as "an inferior woman". With this expression she often wonders why someone with so many social and health difficulties was chosen by *ḍākinīs* as a visionary and as a revealer of treasures. Even though she always felt and saw the presence of the *ḍākinīs* in her life, it took her time and suffering to understand the purpose of it all. She was born in Lhasa in 1892, the first day of the Tibetan Water Dragon year.

She belonged to a very influential family but very quickly began to disagree with her family because they only cared about political power. Since an early age, she demonstrated her interest in a spiritual life, and she had contact with *ḍākinīs* through visions. These clear visionary experiences would mark her destiny.

Sera Khandro's mother died when she was twelve and this was a very important event in her life; she took the decision to abandon her parental house, fleeing from an arranged marriage. She wrote that she ran away from her

---

17 Jacoby, Sarah. H., *Love and Liberation. Autobiographical Writings of the Tibetan Buddhist Visionary Sera Khandro*. Columbia University Press, New York, 2014, p22.

home as if she were escaping from a land of demons. She immediately met a group of religious pilgrims headed by the great master Drimé Ozer.[18] She joined them and instantly developed an intense devotion to the master, and became very close to him. But Drimé Ozer's consort denied her a room in their residence and as some members from the community supported her, Sera had to leave. The woman that once wore beautiful fine clothes started to work as a servant.

Sera Khandro was already a firm practitioner of the path of The Great Perfection[19] and her gifts as a healer and her revelations only increased. She then went to the monastery where Gara Terchen Pema Dundul Wankchuk Lingpa lived, who was a great treasure revealer. Gara Terchen received a prophecy about the healing talents of Sera Khandro and looked for her. However, his consort was hostile towards Sera and their relationship was horrible. During this period, Sera Khandro established a relationship with Gara Terchen's son, Gyelse Pema Namgyel, with whom she had three children, but only the first one, a daughter, lived until adulthood.

This period of Sera Khandro's life was very difficult and turbulent. Her husband disapproved of her activities, especially the fact that she would be a treasure revealer; her husband did not believe in her. Sometimes Sera was unable to walk or travel because of her arthritis, but every time she did not follow the lifestyle revealed in her visions, the consequences impacted directly on her health and consequently her physical body suffered. Dewe Dorje (Blissful Vajra), as Sera Khandro was made known on some occasions, was recognized by some lamas and revealers of treasures as an authentic emanation of Yeshe Tsogyel. Many of them said that she was empowered directly by Padmasambhava. In her writings, Sera Khandro dedicates many pages to describing her encounters with Padmsambhava (whom she generally calls Pema Totrengtsel, which means something like "lotus with the power of the Skull Garland") and with Yeshe Tsogyel. In these meetings, Yeshe Tsogyel especially gave her lessons as well as asked her to comply with the activities and guidelines that were shown.

The period of her relationship with Gyelse came to an end when Sera became seriously ill. Gyelse refused to believe in the reality of her condition when she told him she needed to rest, until some messengers from Drimé Ozer arrived with a message from their teacher that if Sera continued like this, she would die shortly. He certainly did not want to carry the burden of the death of his wife over him, so he recognized that she had to go with Ozer, her true spiritual consort. Also, at that time, Gyelse already had another woman in his life. Drimé Ozer performed rituals and nursed Sera until her complete recovery. Thus, a new period began in her life. Her understanding of her own conditions of life deepened. She understood the importance of having been predestined to be a *terma* revealer and that there were conditions that cannot be modified by human will.

---

18 *Drimé Ozer* (1881-1924). He was a great scholar and *terton*, guru and Sera Kandro´s consort.

19 The *Great Perfection* is considered the central teaching of the Nyigma Tradition and Bon. It is also known as Dzogchen.

The following are words that Sera Khandro received from Yeshe Tsogyel:

> Noblewoman, in order for you to tame beings of the degenerate age, you are the emanation of the enlightened activity of seven *ḍākinīs*. You have been sent out in the form of an insight woman (shes rab mi mo), so secretly take care of beings, and after sixty years I will invite you back here. If you don't follow this crucial point, it will become difficult to maintain the two Treasure teachings in accordance with the *ḍākinīs'* miraculous symbols. Abandon the hustle and bustle of doing many things. If you become attached to this illusory world, don't prepare to stay very long. If you meet someone born in the tiger, monkey, bull, or sheep year, your temporary hindrances will be dispelled. Because everything—disciples, longevity, and Dharma—depends on consorts and doctrine holders, it is imperative that you are careful regarding the crucial point of auspicious connections.[20]

In these words of Yeshe Tsogyel we clearly perceive that the fate of Sera Khandro was clear and well directed towards the intention of being the revealer of divine treasures that would be of great benefit to many types of beings. In her autobiography, Sera expresses that from a very young age she had prophetic dreams, but perhaps the episode that marked the beginning of a great process that would end up transforming her into an authentic spiritual teacher was a trip with her parents to a sacred place dedicated to Padmasambhava. There she had a great revelation and very clear and remarkable visions. Her parents already knew of her contact with *ḍākinīs*, apparently since her birth, but they advised her to keep it a secret.

Due to the purpose of this text, we cannot expand on a detailed explanation and analysis of the treasures that Sera Khandro received, so we will limit ourselves to a brief mention. Our great master was empowered by Vajravarahi[21] in the two cycles of treasure teachings: *The Secret Treasury of Reality ḍākinīs* and *The ḍākinīs' Heart Essence*. Sera would dedicate all of her life to these treasures which through her practices, trips, experiences and visions were expanded upon and clarified. These treasures are composed of many parts, among which we find tantric liturgies, empowerments, explanations about practices, advice and other diverse texts. These treasures would be the basis of Sera Khandro's teachings, which were enriched by the visionary contacts she had with the *ḍākinīs* through lucid dreams. All visionary experience was basically directed by what Sera called the "Guru Couple" (Padmasambhava and his consort Yeshe Tsogyel).

In the following passage we see how Sera received one of her empowerments:

> Yeshé Tsogyel looked after me with great love. She gave

---

20 Jacoby, Sarah. H. *op.cit.*, pp. 96-97.

21 *Vajravarahi*, in Buddhism, is considered a wrathful manifestation of the female Buddha *Vajrayogini*. She is one of the most famous tantric deities in Tibetan Buddhism.

me the golden pages of the fifty-eight-section Dharma cycle Yangsang Khandrö Tuktik, Extremely Secret *ḍākinī*'s Heart Essence, in the manner of oral transmission, and then conferred a symbolic empowerment upon me. She gave me a secret name, Khandro Gyepé Dorjé, and performed the mind-mandate aspiration prayers.[22]

But also, part of the treasures revealed by Sera Khandro were, according to her, findings of material objects in specific places where her visions revealed that she had to go. For example, in her writings she talks about a dream in which Ekajaṭī[23] showed her that the *Three Cycles of Heart Essence* were in a scroll hidden in a woven chest. The deity requested that she remove it on the tenth day of the dragon month and decode the meaning of the symbols on the tenth day of the monkey month. She said that on the tenth day of the dragon month she discovered the Treasure's prophetic guide.[24]

We will finish this brief exposition about the revelations of this remarkable woman by mentioning the importance that the energy centres have in her teachings. In certain ways, attaining spiritual realizations seems to depend on them. This is clearly shown in her writings when she devotes several pages to the subtle channels and the way that energy behaves. One of the most interesting passages dedicated to this is the description in which a great sage and tantric master called Kukkuripa, known as a one of the mahasiddhas,[25] reveals to her in a vivid dream an important teaching about energy channels.

In a synthesized way, Kukkuripa explains that obtaining the highest achievements would be rooted in the purification of the channels, the winds that circulate through them and in the vital nuclei. Purifying the channels implies sealing them with the wind of primordial wisdom; for this, it is necessary to visualize the chakras in the vajra body. According to this sage, from the three main channels through which the energy circulates, five chakras arise. From these chakras emerge channels that are distributed throughout the body, from the head to toe. The essence of the coronary chakra is mirrorlike primordial wisdom; the essence of the throat chakra is discriminating primordial wisdom; the essence of the heart chakra is the expanse of the reality of primordial wisdom; the essence of the navel chakra is the primordial wisdom of sameness and the essence of the secret chakra is the quintessential accomplishment of action of primordial wisdom. In this way, Kukkuripa tells Sera that she must meditate until the chakras and channels appear completely clear. When this happens, awareness is attained.

In ordinary people, these centres are blocked by obscurations coming

---

22 Jacoby, Sarah. H. *op.cit.*, pp. 96.
23 *Ekajaṭī* is one of the *Twenty-one Taras*. She is also known as *Ugra Tara*. She has a fierce aspect and is generally depicted in blue colour. She is one of the main protectors in the Nyigma Tradition.
24 Jacoby, Sarah. H. *op.cit.*, pp. 170-171.

25 *Mahasiddha* is a term that means "master of great accomplishment". The term is applied to someone who attains the sublime *siddhis* through practice and great commitment. It also refers to the eighty-four masters who attained liberation in ancient India.

from different sources, among them and perhaps the most important are the consequences of our own actions and thoughts. It is for this reason that even though primordial energy is present in us, we cannot perceive it and our mundane mind only wanders in the obscurations that keep it blocked. When the energetic mind, which is primordial energy, emerges through the central channel, the karmic winds are extinct. The importance of the points that we have just described, as being central to the revelations of Sera Khandro and which form the basis of her teachings, is reinforced in the following fragment in which the great female *terton* transmits the words received from Yeshe Tsogyel:

> Meditating on channels and winds is the method to bring
>
> your corporeal body of flesh and blood to course in the sky.
>
> If you are able to mix the wind and mind as one,
>
> your activities as an accomplished master will be without reversal.[26]

When we read about Sera Khandro, it is almost impossible not to remember the visionary experiences of the German Christian mystic Hildegard of Bingen. Both were women who, living in different historical times and circumstances, shared the consequences of their visionary experiences. In both, the visions had the function of revealing knowledge or forms of interpretation that could open the mind of people to deeper realities. Hildegard as well as Sera suffered in their physical body the intensity of their visionary processes. Sera Khandro suffered from arthritis aggravated by her life's conditions and the effect of her illness seemed to be increased when she did not follow the advice of her visions. Hildegard suffered from intense headaches that often took her away from her daily tasks. But, despite all of that, they succeeded in granting to us the wonderful and priceless legacy of their wisdom. In 1940 Sera Khandro left this world to become the true essence of her own teachings.

Bibliography:

Chagdud Rinpoche, Tulku. *Gates to Buddhist Practice.* Ed. Padma Publishing. USA, 1993.

Doney, Lewis. *Padmasambhava in the Conjured Past.*

Jacoby, Sarah. H. *Love and Liberation. Autobiographical Writings of the Tibetan Buddhist Visionary Sera Khandro.* Ed. Columbia University Press, New York, 2014.

Mishra, Umakant. *Searching for the Lotus pond of Dhanakosha of Guru Rinpoche (Padmasambhava)–An alternative approach from the Archaeology of Buddhism in Orissa.*

Norbu, Thinley. *The Small Golden Key. To the Treasure of the Various Essential Necessities of General and Extraordinary Buddhist Dharma.* Ed. Shambhala, USA, 1993.

Rinpoche, Dudjom. *The Nyigma School of Tibetan Buddhism. Its Fundamentals & History.* Translated by Gyurme Dorje and Mattew Kapstein. Ed. Wisdom Publications, USA, 1991.

---

26 Jacoby, Sarah. H. *op.cit.*, pp. 82.

Simmer-Brown, Judith. *Ḍākinīs's Warm Breath. The Feminine Principle in Tibetan Buddhism.* Ed. Shambhala. USA, 2002.

Shaw, Miranda. *Buddhist Goddesses of India.* Ed. Princeton University Press, Oxford.

Thondup Rinpoche, Tulku. *Hidden Teachings of Tibet. An Explanation of the Terma Tradition of Tibetan Buddhism.* Edited by Harold Talbott. Ed. Wisdom Publications, USA, 1997.

https://approachingaro.org/terma-validation-in-practice
https://www.britannica.com/
https://www.rigpawiki.org/

by Moonlight as Sun

Musson

The alchemical mixture of sun, rain and seed in the womb of the earth provides us with the simple pleasure and necessity of nourishment. Food is magic, and cookery a form of sorcery. Without nourishment humanity would perish in an apocalyptic descent of mass starvation and suffering. 75,000 years ago the golden wheat crop that we see growing in numerous fields today had its simple origins with a group of wild grasses called Triticeae. Cultivation of wheat crops took place over 10,000 years ago and originated from the wild grasses found growing in rich abundance upon the land. This simple change not only in diet but in raising arable crops changed the nomad and hunter lifestyle to that of farmer. The golden wheat and barley crops were the first cereals known to have been domesticated by our early ancestors and it is from these early times that man first discovered the secret of seed germination.

 The human race has been digesting gluten and starch as a main staple since the domestication of wild grasses. Today in our postmodern world some 10,000+ years later, we are eating the same simple food groups that nourished our forefathers. The human body needs proteins, fats and carbohydrates with a dash of vitamins and minerals to maintain optimal health. Was it by chance or grand design that the natural hybridisation between two wild grasses, einkorn and emmer, gave early man another food group to choose from and establish a settled lifestyle? Add these basics to the early invention of cooked food from grains that have been parched, simmered or ground and you can start to see the origin and rise of nourishment, health and longevity. The brain receives carbohydrates, it develops further and so begins the journey of thoughts, ideas and beliefs. A plentiful food supply gave the opportunity for real development, growth and the start of settled civilisation.

As agriculture came to dominate daily life, so too did the Gods and Goddesses that protected the fields and gave bountiful harvests. Intergenerational families passed down magic and ritual in the spring planting and summer harvest rites. Fertility had a supernatural element associated with it. The importance of cooking the harvested grains was also surrounded by much rural folklore and superstition. Early European culture suggests that the making of daily bread holds ancient belief in dragons. The winged snakes of the sky taught our ancestors how to plough the earth, sow, grow, reap and bake bread from the grains. The belief of the common folk is that bread is a gift from the Gods and so plays vital roles in yearly celebrations of life and death. It is the staff of life. The baking and breaking of bread with one's family and friends not only shows social status but also unites all in the community. Later Christianity can clearly be seen to filter through into the same folk beliefs and the old Gods become devils and demons. The sky serpents are blamed for morally leading astray the people and corrupting them with the lavish recipes of rich cakes, breads and pastries. The brewing of alcohol is even seen as the Devil's work! Bread becomes the body of the saviour and the alcoholic grain beverage becomes red wine to mimic the suffering Lord's blood in the new religion.

Famine, pestilence, epidemics, war and eventual starvation were constant fears throughout history. So too was crop failure due to inclement weather or natural disaster. Such occurrences would certainly mean lean times on the dinner plate and, come the winter months, mass starvation. In a period of good harvest, all grains grown would, with correct storage and pest control, last considerably longer than any dried meats, fruit or vegetable stock. Grain also as a raw ingredient was the basis of the people's diet who relied upon it not only for the daily bread but also a flagon of ale. In a harsh winter, grain stocks could run dangerously low. The safety of spring with better weather and a fresh growing season did nothing to help hungry bellies; the harvest had to last. When people are starving as recorded on the European continent in 1500s, grain flour was substituted for or diluted with acorn flour or tree bark, tiles, bricks and even dried bones (animal or human) all ground down and baked to help delay the process of hunger and eventual starvation. The bread most certainly did not taste nice and would have had poor if little nutritional value, but it was the only option in times of utter crisis. So the golden grains of harvest became worth more than any gold.

Historically whole empires have risen and fallen due to the necessity of a plentiful supply of food. Sacrifice and appeasement to ancient Gods gave security both on a spiritual and material level. Votive offerings entwined with historic intergenerational beliefs gave people of many different cultures and lands a generic solution to the fear of hunger. From Ashnan, the Mesopotamian goddess of grain to Žemyna, the Lithuanian mother-goddess of agriculture and a fertile earth, the nourishment given by grain gods the world over, in every aeon, culture and landscape gave bounty to obedient subjects.

The Egyptian empire and later the legends of that land portray Osiris and Isis as the Gods that showed the people the cultivation of wheat and barley crops. Tevnut and Rem were also worshiped for the fertile growing rains and moisture given upon the lands. In Babylon we have Ishtar and later her son, Tammuz. He became the spirit of the corn, a young God who died each year and yet returned to life again. This ancient myth also resembles that of the Greek goddess of the corn, Demeter, and her daughter Persephone whose journeying into the underworld symbolises the mysteries associated with birth and death. Much later we have the Aztec priests who notoriously performed sacrificial blood rites to feed and nourish the earth in order for abundant maize and legume harvests. The severing of the head from the body or the ripping out of a human heart were especially favoured along with the slicing of main arteries around the body. Blood was the ultimate fertiliser for the land and such Gods as Acan, Axomamma, Chicomecoatl, Pachamama, Sara Mama and Xipe Totec demanded much human blood. It is still a practice in certain magics to feed a plant or the soil it grows in with drops of blood to strengthen the spell. Words without blood, it is said, are just air so will not work. The plant once harvested contains much more power, be it is used for healing or hexing. Crops grown over historical battle and war zones clearly show that the blood and the decaying human bodies enrich the soil and provide a plentiful source of nutrients.

When sacrificial victims, either human or animal, became scarce or beliefs changed throughout the lands, smaller handmade idols were created as the sacrificial symbols made for the Gods and land spirits. Clay figures and later plaited straw with grains attached from either the first or last cut of harvest would be made to house and appease deities and the believed spirit of the crop. In each land and continent around the world symbols and amulets would be produced from the growing crop and saved safely in the hope for a good harvest in the next year. Corn dollies and spirits are not just rural crafting but magical talismans and idols that are as individual to a landscape and region as a person's own fingerprints. The ancient yearly tradition was to take the corn and create a dwelling place for the spirit whilst in the field. Each farming family made their own Corn Maiden, Mother or Grandmother and this was traditionally the job of the eldest male or female farmer on the family land. Indeed the very earth upon which the crop is grown has a name given by the farmer or past landowner. This name rarely changes and can be traced in records going back hundreds of years. Some old maps held by British churches clearly show parish boundaries and also state the names of the fields. This I believe is for when the Christian church performed the old rite of Rogation, the blessing of the crops for a bountiful harvest. Sadly this is not a ritual that is widely seen today in rural parishes due to austerity cut-backs. It bought villager and church dignitaries together in a wonderful ritual of blessing the land within the parish. I miss this tradition and ritual ceremony, as so too do I miss seeing the old ways which are becoming lost to modern scientific means. The connection to the earth and land is special and it is a living breathing being.

Sacrificial blood has now been replaced by chemical fertilisers in agriculture. The old ancient practice of blood sacrifice still symbolically survives in our modern world and the traditional harvest crafts of yesteryear play an important role in keeping the heritage alive. Notice the magical and devotional element has been turned into a folk revival .The simple plaited odd-looking straw dollies made from either the first cut of corn or last, are the bastions of this ancient tradition. The red ribbon used to decorate the straw work represents the life blood, both given and taken as sacrifice. Other colours are used by crafters but the true traditional ribbon

is a rich bright red that contrasts beautifully with the gold of the cereal straw. This is a sacrificial remembrance of the ancient blood rite and one that still lives on today albeit only aesthetically. Red works best for reasons deeply embedded in the human psyche – a tradition not quite fully remembered, but also not quite fully forgotten. Can these iconic straw effigies be traced to the Greek goddess of the corn, Demeter?

Ancient antiquity records Demeter as the corn mother and the goddess crowned upon and in the harvest field, with corn puppets or dollies made in her form. But these strange plaited straw emblems have an ancient tradition in many other distant lands. All countries and people celebrated the safe gathering in of cereal crops, and made as offerings to the land and spirits a home for them to retreat and dwell in. A male and female fertility spirit was captured and kept safe throughout the winter months, only to be released either by fire or ploughing back into the land once the spring months came. Many traditions similarly state a field once harvested goes through a violent death; sacred edible seeds are kept safe to be reborn. A yearly cycle of ploughing, sowing and reaping represents the life of a man and woman. The spirit of the crop retreats inside the first and last cut of a field, and to show honour and respect for the lifesaving nourishment of the grains it is transformed into an amulet or effigy for keeping the spirit alive – a peculiar kind of spirit in the grain akin to a jinn in a magical lamp that will always provide sustenance. The corn dollie becomes the outcome of the harvest and of many future harvests to come. The plaited straw is the offering given instead of the blood and death rite of centuries past. There are many variations the world over for the traditions of sowing and reaping cereal crops and sadly these are becoming forgotten and lost traditions. Food and its production must never be taken for granted. Science may have replaced the Gods of agriculture and earth, but man's stupidity and high regard for money and the atomic number 79 over the health of the land will prove fatal. We live in times of greed when food really is running at a surplus to requirements and is kept in such abundance to satisfy our appetites. The supermarket shelves of plenty are there for your choice if only you can afford the prices.

In our unbalanced postmodern western world we have heart disease, obesity and type two diabetes in the majority of the population. Each and every one of us can live like Henry the Eighth and surround ourselves with mass quantities of food and drink. We are literally surrounded by a gluttony of food that is constantly thrown away due to sell-by dates and lack of consumers. Our survival rate is high as we consider ourselves infallible; we are comfortable with sophisticated and technological advancements. Our smart phones have all the answers. We Google ancient deities and visit museums as the altars and temples are no longer in existence to worship at. Something deep down in our human subconscious still understands the ancient origins of food and grain worship and we fear hunger. Indeed most of us carry a few extra pounds of bonus weight that we pay excessive sums to loose through dieting clubs.

The magical wheel of the year has become one big artificial sweetener of mass consumption. Our celebrations and sacred harvesting have all globally merged into one excessive production line. Food and sacredness no longer correlate. We

are becoming confused in our artificial world of marketing posters *vs* nature and the natural environment. Our ancestors ate with the natural flow and ebb of the seasons. From peasants to lords, diets it could be argued were considerably healthier without the addition of E numbers, aspartame or trans fats that prolong the shelf life of goods or substitute as sugars. Simple foods suited simple body types and not a lot has changed in the evolution of the human body and its processing of food groups. Breads, cakes, pastries or pies were the gold return of the summer harvest and still are along with the ale and other alcoholic beverages made from grains. The true magic and joy of simple foods in season is being lost with twenty-four-hour delivery and availability of our ever-demanding postmodern world.

Farming and the gathering in of the harvest may not be a primary hi-tech industry that captures the hearts of a young population obsessed with Xbox games or indeed hold much magical interest for those only absorbed in high-brow ritual magic. The ancient golden grain production simply equates to survival and that for me personally is a magical act. Unless you are coeliac or mildly intolerant you will consume this ancient substance on a daily basis. Rice, maize, wheat, barley, rye, oats and spelt are some of the oldest grains that humanity continues to consume. The old Gods are still with us and most definitely still linger upon the land and so become consumed in our bodies. We eat our Gods even if we don't sacrifice or pay homage to them as our ancestors did. The soil holds the secrets of past worship and fertility. We have become fragmented from the soils of our lands and our individual cultural heritage has eroded as we have become seduced by highly processed food with brightly coloured packaging. Take away the artificial preservatives and you will find the true nourishment of the land. The rich gold of multiple harvests and the healing energy of simple food without modern interference is the back-to-basics and ancient idealism we are in need of and hungry for. The magic is in the simplicity of soil and so in our food as we eat our Gods. The more the land is molested the more sick its people become.

The real gold is in the fields, not locked away in bank vaults. It grows and ripens as much by sun as moonlight. Without it, whole countries would be in crisis, but it is all too readily taken for granted. We really need to get back to basics not only with our governmental leadership but with our own magical systems. We are so strongly connected to the soil, our earth; as in Arthurian legend, 'The King and the land are one'. Alanis Obomsawin, an Abenaki from the Odanak reserve in the 1970s spoke the immortal words … "When the last tree is cut, the last fish is caught, and the last river is polluted; when to breathe the air is sickening, you will realise too late, that wealth is not in bank accounts and that you can't eat money."

The real power and magic is in the natural world and this connects everyone and everything. I am not personally against the scientific progression of an industry or people; I'm no luddite. But I do think the loss of a connection to the land and the commodity market has resulted in a new disaffected generation and a people lacking identity and spiritual fulfilment. Let's not worship the false artificial sweetener gods anymore but return to the arms of our ancestors and all take care of the land and so in return our own bodies.

GUNS OF BRIXTON

> SOMETIMES THINGS ARE REAL WHETHER YOU WANT THEM TO BE OR NOT.

ANTHONY NINE

When they kick at your front door it's already too late. Unmarked meatwagon tire screech outside the building and jackboot footsteps falling in the hallway. We've had all our dress rehearsals.

Want to know a real secret of magic? Some motherfucker is always going to try to claim your misfortune as their result. Let's not give our attention to clickbait commentators who have never been on the court themselves serving up hot takes on the dark science of alt-right meme magic. Let's not participate in enflaming a narrative that fawns over and rewards the keyboard antics of stunted men nursing misplaced grievance and kicking it down the line to the usual suspects. That's an old cowardice, and it's not the first time it's been dressed up in boot boy chic.

Cartoon frogs and reheated chaos magic didn't put the mad king on the throne. There's no glory in glitchy, mean-spirited spells ringing out like a fourth-generation copy of a Death in June record taped from the library in 1986. If half-arsed chaos magic moves could remake reality so effortlessly, we would have been inhabiting a cheap amphetamine and White Lightning cider-based utopia for decades now – trust me. Don't mistake a symptom for a cause.

Sorcerers scry into rancid roadside pools though, and this is no different. Take a hard look at that smirking, flatulent amphibian visage leering back at you out of jpeg sortilege. It was never a spell. This is a mirror trained upon our own filth. All of the foul compulsions that our better instincts push down into arduous basements and stinking cellars. Wet-nursed in submerged enclaves and reared to snarling manifestation under a climate where capacity for empathy and compassion are eroded and made to seem untenable.

Cruelty raised as a virtue, enthroned and imperceptibly normalized over time. Cultivated in increments until you're ready to cheer on the abominable. Howling laughter at toddlers snatched from their loved ones and trafficked into cages. Mockery of violated women, dragged over hot coals, brutalized and unheard. Shattered crowds gleefully tormented further for nihilist comedy value. If all of this had a face, you know what it would look like. Amphibian doppelgänger marching in step on the reverse of the mirror.

Sequestered in solitary citadels squat would-be wicked wizards. Receivers of a shriveled transmission that lingers and lures in malcontented foot soldiers. Black shirt propagandists employing the method of Leeds and Stoke Newington towards purposes never intended. Sour spells seeping imperceptible into the spectacle and seeding mistrust. Rupturing consensus world-views into a constellation of poisoned shards and misshapen fragments.

Damaged spyglass observation and shattered magic mirror revelation create a landscape of treacherous splinters. Polluted clouds obscuring a true course through turbulent waters. Seven of Cups delirium stirred to a crescendo and weaponized to undermine even the possibility for such a course. Fertile soil for the slow dead pulse of cruel hypnosis sent like a signal. Persistent attrition wearing down all defense against insidious broadcast and anti-life equation.

Infected by contagious narrative and invited to swim in polluted waters, it could be easy to mistake such insidious enchantments for the whole terrain of magic. A sea of misinformation and subterfuge sailed upon by upstart startup pirates.

Sometimes there will be an evil mastermind inside a volcano lair who has built a contraption that can influence the weather, but he is not the storm. The sea and the dead it contains don't shift their tides for a deft hypnotist. Seeds sprout in the dirt and grow in a writhing pattern without a thought to what song might be on the radio. Roots of your being have pushed up through malignant soil such as this before.

PRESS-GANGED

A plain white candle and a glass of water for your dead is a revolutionary act when your dead have been forcibly suppressed. Hostages shut away in cold murk for a thousand years or more. Sometimes scratching at you in dreams or a thin voice choked by rolling banks of fog dense with lumbering shapes.

The first thing they always take is the dirt under your feet. Sterilize the cities and the villages of their walking stones and haunted ends. Evict the troll under the bridge and knacker the skeleton horse. Make alterations to old maps and print new ones more conducive to extracting a profit from your labour.

Turgid wand conjures disconnected globules of flesh estranged from the momentous pulse and churn of bone and spirit. Shunted around streets that you can't feel soaked in history that you've forgotten. Then they come for your dead, to undermine any firm foundation of resistance that you might cleave to.

Lock it all down and shape a world where nobody even believes in their dead anymore. Give it a few centuries and you start to think it had been your own idea all along. They don't even have to criminalise it. Those who forget the past are easier to rob of a future. Drive a wedge in deep so that you start to splinter and you can't feel the towering mounds of ghost flesh winding back out of you into the fabric of time.

Make that condition permanent. Get them comfortable with it. Export it until it takes hold in every hold-out and outpost that remembers. Push it out to the furthest reaches where you are certain it will wither and die, but it doesn't. Mothers give birth to children who can still hear, and the act of remembering itself becomes a weapon.

Don't get it twisted. There is profit to be made in selling a false idea of your ancestors back to you. You get malleable when the roots are cut from under you. Predators will sniff out the wound and offer to sop it up with something ancestor-shaped of their own fabrication.

Peddling you the Netflix version of your own dead, portrayed as mighty Vikings or knights in shining armour. All the while prying you further and further away from the lived reality of your material ancestors. Blood of your blood, all dentures and Dettol and dying in debt.

Courageous unglamorous lives that shaped your substance and the labyrinthine tangle of one another that expresses itself as the contemporary moment. It's in this ownership of who you are, and how you came to be that way, in all its difficult human complexity, that strong ancestral foundations may be cultivated.

Vague rhetorical hand-waving in the direction of something you remember from storybooks is not the same as putting in the hours at the white table. Incremental tending feeds the fractured foundations, cultivates a spiritual base, orients you within a broader world of spirit.

Skip that or swap it out for bullshit, and you risk getting led by the nose on tiki torch parades. Stomping your feet about blood and soil, on soil drenched in the blood of the dead that you and yours have wronged.

There are many strategies for repairing the ancestral disconnect, administering to chronic symptoms of neglect and orienting to the new cognisance that follows immersion in this work. Cultivate a magic that assembles itself upon this basic reality of our physical prehistory – and how it has shaped our nature and circumstance – and your magic starts to move with the weight of the dead behind it.

Sorcery begins to feel less like a fickle shopping list of spells. All inconstant longing and half-baked intentions swarming upon you like a cloud of maybes. Hit and miss wishes thrown up like paper planes in the hope that something might stick.

Step in time with the dead and the whole ancestral structure begins to move as one. Casting your magic from the summit of the bone mountain that supports you, not like a clammy fist blasting out its wants into a swamp of assumption.

Roots of the self bound in with roots of all life, interconnected and entwined within the greater structure. The depth of our reach into the dense soil of the dead intensifying the tremors of intent. Conjured signal ringing out like a tuning fork through labyrinthine branches of being. Skeleton trees crowded together in thick bramble and blessed thicket. Plants that whisper to bone and blood. Dirt that speaks. The stories that the forest tells itself and who will write them.

As the substance of our connection to the full complex ancestral tree is vivified through a practice, so will our intentions and the direction of our work become more readily attuned to the healthy functioning of the whole organism as it exists in time.

Reflections of this idea are everywhere, and there are many expressions of the same impulse to incorporate one's dead into the contemporary moment and grow in the optimal direction with the potency of its weight.

There is also magic that doesn't nourish or pay mind to this foundational point, assembling itself upon compelling yet less certain ground. Magic that can tie you up for decades cataloguing footnotes on the unclear purpose of an unfinished pattern. Magic that was never what it purported to be, and sought to mislead from the vacuum of its failing with inscrutable terminology and spaghetti alphabet shapes.

Magic that feels like having walked into a terrible coke room at a party and not being able to find the way out. Magic that mistakes jockeying for status in delusional social clubs for the elusive door, and turns a blind eye to predators under its roof if they will shore up its insecurity. Magic that rides on the coat tails of past days, either someone else's or its own.

Magic that sets itself up as a storefront but does not attend to the ruin and injustice within its own orbit. Magic that takes PayPal and worries about its Instagram following but has faltered in its purpose with the passing of years.

Magic that plays the con and has got comfortable bending its integrity when it has bills to pay. Magic that's always on the take and passing it off as something else. Magic with its hand in the till.

Magic that wears white but isn't something that should. Magic that wears black and thinks it's something it isn't. Magic that doesn't want to bother. Magic that won't look in the hardest places or accept what it sees there. Magic that is coming up right now and is pressed to navigate the scope of this terrain.

DISOBEDIENCE

The malefica in play does not obscure its intentions or functioning. Like a Bond villain revealing the plan while you're strapped to a steel table, it is not difficult to follow the method and grasp the desired outcome as you watch the laser beam inch its way closer between your legs.

Cast amid a formidable hall-of-mirrors-spell intended to exhaust critical faculties *en masse* via a flooding torrent of alternative perspectives. Gaming our biology by saturating cognitive functions to their limit with an endless stream of weaponized opinions and manipulative glamours. Running a straight-up numbers game until something snaps under the wearying onslaught of conflicting and confusing narrative. A withering curse set upon our collective sense of what's real until it simply buckles and gives out.

Evil science can be dug up and sent back though, and not everything is so easily persuaded that it isn't real. Sometimes things are real whether you want them to be or not.

Shift the terrain to your advantage wherever possible. Don't allow your opponent to meet you on their choice of ground if it can be avoided. This is not something to be fought with rival memes or any iteration of the same shabby playbook. Change the circumstances of the game ahead of the first move and catch the aggressor on the back foot.

It can begin very simply with small acts. A cup of water and a plain white candle. The incorporation of one's dead into the contemporary moment. Cultivating visceral experience of oneself as the tip of a branch on a literal tree of life made of everything that has ever lived. Awareness of the fluid of the dead that permeates the living world and the grace to navigate its saltwater seas and sunken depths.

Perceive the city, or wherever your footsteps fall, from the same ancestral vantage point. Thick sediment of dead down cobblestone ends. The tall house with too many attics. Ghostlife congregating at the crossroads. Enflame the vision to inhabit sideways versions of place. A hagstone window to witness splendours of time.

Learn the topography that you see about you in this vision. Know where the haunted ponds and lonely canals are, and what lives under certain hills. Develop a familiarity with the crossroads of import that you pass by everyday, and the principal intersections of your town. Get to know their flavour and the dead that walk there. Establish yourself upon this point by some means.

Know where the nearest patch of woods is, but do not go foolhardily into the forest or drink freely from sumptuous banquet tables one may find. Learn the etiquette and the safeguards. Make the right tributes and develop some trust. Cunning isn't a title. You are either actively cunning in the course of your magic, or you diminish in some regard. Keep it sharp.

Spend time with mermaids. Go frequently to the closest body of water, and encounter its presence as a replenishing force within nature. Observe how this character and presence may change when you meet it at different points along its course. Get how the undine of an underground river is unlike wildwater mermaids of the river rapids.

Give prayer and silver coins to Mary Star of the Sea, but court her daughters at your own risk. Scry into the shoreline and read auguries in the patterns made by seaweed, driftwood and the fruits of the sea. Learn to pay attention to spirit to such a degree that a magic of place assembles itself. Ways of seeing, a living formulary, tools gifted from the deep.

Follow the track of the corpse road to its lychgate and make good at the door. See the cemetery for what it is, without a spooky overlay absorbed from b-movies and Halloween specials. Wet the beak of the boneyard rulers, but don't push too far too fast. Get to know who is buried in the graves, and how their character shapes the politics of each burial ground, but don't make any assumptions. Slow and steady wins the race in the day and hour of Saturn.

Exist with awake awareness within the living process of nature and let it reveal what it will teach. Take your holy water from the May rainfall, and inhabit the righteousness of blazing fire when you set a light upon a work. Cultivate kinship with the wild things that grow and employ them as sibling not commodity.

Listen so closely that you can feel the turn of the earth below your feet, and know the tide of the moon without looking. Extend that sense outwards to encompass the placement of the Earth within the solar system, its rotation and journey around the sun, and the terrestrial mysteries of that process that are marked and dramatised in festival and saint's day. Further still to other celestial bodies and the gravity they exert upon the moment.

In the fullness of this contemplation, witness the pulse of life that imbues this whole system, which is as much as we need to or can know about the Divine. Immanence in nature is tracked in maps that chart the relationship between the brilliant light and the solidity of matter. A literal tree of life, composed of all living things and all things that have ever lived within time, interpenetrated by grace. Abstract creator within creation cross-sectioned like the layers of an onion. Emanations of spirit refracted like laser beams or a vivid spectrum of mystery. This sense of creator within creation has emanations by which we may seek to understand its abstract divinity.

Magic always has consequences one way or another. Observed from the outside, much of this practice will look like results-oriented sorcery, firmly focused on worldly practicalities and survival needs. Fixing remedies, performing cleansings, telling

fortunes, divining for stolen property, protecting from harm, bringing justice.

Yet the work of it – the ways of seeing that are developed, the relationships with spirit that are formed, and the points upon which you are strengthened – will act upon you. Magic will change you if you're doing it right. It won't take complacency or let you remain within a comfort zone for long. If you're not having that dynamic motion as a characteristic of your involvement in magic over time, and remain largely unchanged and unaffected by your activities in this sphere, then a Roger Moore eyebrow might be raised.

The transformative process of the work can play out in many ways, but when you begin experiencing the collective dead and entirety of living nature as a single organism affected by celestial tides and imbued with divinity, and then ground that into your daily life through sorcerous action, the result is no less mystical than other methods that place their mysticism more front and centre.

Our situation is that such complex animist perspectives or world views have largely been erased so that others may profit. A stitch-up spread like a viral infection with colonialism as its carrier agent. Magic held fast in the landscape though. There are no territories where it did not in some form. Even at ground zero, where these enclosures were first set in place, magic persisted.

CROOKED

The magic of Europe is a fractured line of transmission. A shattered road that will disappear for some sections and then appear again somewhere else entirely. A treacherous walk that will confound its traveller in its forking paths, curious byways and forbidding lanes.

It is not any one thing. A tidy lineage with all its paperwork in order, or a suppressed folk religion. It's Elizabethan scholar and renegade priest, militant midwife and Jack-the-Lad chancer. It doesn't fit together very easily, and you have to piece it together out of the field notes of shady conjurors navigating by cut-up grimoires copied-out by hand, or get it from outraged clerics penning stern warnings not to do it.

It keeps its hood up against the night for a few decades, simmering under the radar, then blisters up in theatrical Egyptian headgear and funny handsigns. It sets up shop in Cafe Royal and Rabellaisian Abbey, Romany caravan and Hackney squat.

It doesn't sit still for very long. It can mug you with Trans-Yuggothian interludes or bring you white hot visions of the hawk that rends the world. It can try to remember parts of itself, and reinvent them with naked blood-letting and rope bondage. It can listen to the dirt and what it brings.

It can look outside itself, over the seas, because that too is a mystery of which it partakes. It can blunder in and start helping itself. It can try to cobble together its own sandbox versions of the magic of other lands through guesswork and intuition, or it can try to fill in the blanks of a reconstructed practice by plugging in garbled bootlegs of experiential mysteries it has only read about in books.

In all of these endeavors, it is trying to address something that is missing. Components of itself that it half-remembers but no longer has a roadmap for. Some means of adjusting the volume to better hear the insistent voices of land and dead that stir its memory. It can pretend torturous history never happened and be in denial about the ancestral tensions bound around such dialogue, or it can take ownership of the footsteps of its dead and where they have trodden.

If this is your dead, then no matter where you may choose to pour out an offering of rum, you will always be doing so at the fraught crossroads where the magic of Europe, of its landscape and suppressed spirits, encounters the magic of the lands that its empires have colonised.

We can talk about re-enchanting or re-wilding the landscape as a strategy of resistance, but unless we're also being honest about why a re-enchantment is required, where such toxic disenchantment began and how it proliferated – then it's just another spiritual Brexit.

There are few deals to be had with spirits of the woods who remember exactly who it was that slew their oak forests and turned them into slave ships. There are no bargains to be made with water, soiled and ravaged, and coming to drown you. You can't navigate the Far Lands when you don't know which treaties have been broken and which grievances are being concealed until it's too late.

There is no reconciliation to be found with the immensity of the tree. Thick roots in the underworld, branches comprising all life, subject to seasons and imbued with spirit. Without attempting to be fully conscious upon this point. Accepting the cost of blood and hearing the intranquil dead. Making a decision about which side of the road you're going to stand on.

Blackshirt jugglers try to lay an ahistoric racial claim on your landscape and its folklore, but they don't deal in the reality of it. They want you hermetically sealed off in ethnically segregated mythospheres that are easy to police. Encouraging flight into an idyllic pastoral delusion demarcated by spurious notions of whiteness that have only ever been a control system.

Setting up barricades around concepts of ancestral lineage that they get to define, and which never account for the slippery unpredictability of how babies are made and have been made through the unfathomable expanse of time. Exploiting a yearning for lost mythic landscape, without understanding that such things are not static or located in an idealised past, but present and dynamic. Woven thick with life and saturated in the dead of their haunts.

Place exists in relationship to place. Akin to how flowers are polinated by the activity of insects. Cities grow in relation to other cities as a result of the traffic that they see. The roads trodden between them over time and the spells walked into them for good or ill. The shifting patterns of immigration that shape the character of a place over generations and become a part of its mysteries.

The great forests of Europe didn't vanish on their own. Enchanted wood felled and crafted into dreadful fleets. Dispatched far and wide loaded with terrible cargo. Wild spaces hacked away to nothing and repurposed as undead vessels of psychic infection bound for undiscovered terrain. If you are looking for the lost magical landscape of England, that's where it went. All roads lead to the same unresolved crossroads sooner or later.

TIGHTEN UP

Yet what rude beast slouches towards Coldharbour Lane to be born? Conceived in a hostile environment and brought to term beneath the heel of austerity. Nightbus nativity under a Brixton sun. Crossbones flag swaddling covers the glare so that spirit may pass. *Se li ki pote drapo, se li ki a pare soley pou Lwa yo.*

It should never feel like a renactment. We're supposed to build on what our ancestors created and take it further in a way that serves the future, not golden age their struggle or settle for diminished expectations.

Anyone with half a head for this can hear the accusatory voices of the future dead. Clawing at you out of the worst timeline through the substance of the tree. Bitter ghosts of Christmases yet to come, weeping and wailing outside of time.

Magic is of little use if it does not provide a window of hope. However dire a situation, magic is there to give you a way to play the angles and create a more favourable outcome than what might transpire if problematic circumstances were left unchecked. It's not wallowing in powerlessness and the pornography of doom. Its game is called surviving. As in heaven, as in hell.

Consider the nature of the spell that you are casting. Not just on a given day, but in the broad sweep of your work. Every act adds up and accumulates to a pattern. You don't want to have to look back and not like the stitches you have made, or have to unravel difficult knots that should never have been tightened.

Magic can be brought to act around any willed intention, and could be seen as a means of shaping, refining and nourishing that intention. You can frequently tell how much of this work a person has likely done from the way that they will talk about it. Portrayals that present magic as too powerful to use, lending you an unfair advantage, or only to be rolled out as a last resort, invariably betray a hypothetical sense of its operating parameters. Sometimes occultists like to feed and maintain an empowering image of their own magical potency, while carefully avoiding any actions that might challenge or undermine the integrity of that house of cards.

Like martial artists who have never been in a real fight or had any live experience outside of a controlled setting, there is a certain rude awakening that comes from bringing this work into a real world sphere in all its complexity and unpredictability. Not as a casual or occasional solution when all else has failed, but as your integral response to everyday turbulence. Magic as a condensation of the choices you make and a means of enflaming a given need to material fruition. Magic not as something extra or added, but as an organic and artful response to circumstance, and a medium for shaping and cultivating what takes place within your orbit.

There are frequently unique variables in play that are specific to a given situation, and which must be anticipated or navigated by divinatory inquiry for the work to land correctly and without adverse or unforeseen repercussions. This process of peering deeply into a turbulent predicament and assessing its potential vectors of manifestation can yield much value in itself, irrespective of what you may then choose to do with that information.

Miraculous-seeming shit can go down in magic, but it's rarely just a matter of waving a hazel wand. Sometimes a situation has already progressed too far to turn it around, or your work just doesn't have sufficient leverage or reach to manifest with the desired impact. Sometimes alternative angles of approach must be devised, or preliminary operations required in order to provide an opening for later work or offset the risk of unintended side effects.

All of these considerations become instinctive through repetition of the practice. You start to get a feel for this terrain and can often see the various possible trajectories and potential pitfalls inherent in a planned work at the outset, and make whatever adjustments or contingencies may be required as you devise a strategy. Much of this nuance is obfuscated, if not invisible to someone coming to it cold.

There is nothing wrong with lighting a candle for world peace and works of that ilk. The foundation practice of various expressions of Spiritism contain batteries of prayers for the uplifting and elevation of all. Sometimes the most general petition sent out in every direction can exert its magnetism and deliver an intended result. Easy magic should never be overlooked or underestimated.

Yet if we are to bring that general impact magic out of its sphere and expect it to conjure very specific, distant or difficult results, then our potential for success starts to feel compromised. This is frequently an impending flaw in many well-intentioned efforts at political magic, which can risk squandering the energy and enthusiasm poured into them due to problematic delivery.

Works that have hobbled themselves before they get out the door due to a faulty premise. When you only ever roll out sorcery for special occasions, like a moth-eaten suit dug out for job interviews and funerals, there is a good chance that you might misjudge the distance, swing and miss.

While it is circumspect not to be too attached to any particular expectation of how your results may play out, and to always build in free space for the unforseen and unexpected, it also pays to give some thought to what your results might look like and what sort of practical real world outcome might reasonably constitute success.

The notion of attempting to "bind" a person, as opposed to simply cursing them, has much currency among would-be witches squeamish about the potential consequences of their attempted sorcerous action. As strategies go, there is perhaps something more honest about a straight-up curse. Like a swift, heartfelt punch to the nose, you're expressing a simplicity of intent that knows what it is about and isn't pretending to be anything else or trying to weasel around the consequences of its actions. If you're going to do something in magic, own it. Inhabit it and commit to it, instead of complicating its trajectory with imagined caveats and loopholes.

There is little basis in folk magic for a generic "binding", along the lines of the term's contemporary deployment. You might bind up someone's mouth to stop gossip, or bind the hands of a domestic abuser, or bind a person to complete a specific task. But the idea of binding someone from doing "all harm", as it is commonly framed, is a curious proposition when you try to picture it unfolding. We do harm somewhere as individuals all the time under late stage capitalism, let alone if we were a politician or world leader, whose every ill-considered policy move or spiteful 3am tweet carries ramifications for someone.

Binding such a figure from doing any harm at all is a hard target, and the likelihood of landing it with scattershot process doesn't feel too great. Certainly those odds go up if you have enough people throwing at the same target at the same time, but probably not exponentially. There is also an undercurrent of hubris to the expectation that burning a spell candle every month would be enough to upend a political regime. It's hard to imagine that such solutions would not have already been tried by people steeped in less dislocated magical cultures than ours, who nevertheless remain subject to authoritarian government.

Another complicating factor is the difficulty of getting a clear fix on a target without access to their personal concerns such as hair or nail clippings. A photograph or handwritten signature is a poor substitute for grasping something of the target, especially if you are attempting to extend your reach to impact someone who is not personally known to you. It's also prudent to be wary of spells that are so nebulous in their intent that almost anything could be seized upon as proof of a result. This is another of the problems attached to vague, all-encompassing outcomes without a clear criteria of accomplishable change. There is too much scope to be dishonest with oneself about what might constitute the success of such a work.

If you catch yourself speculating about how much worse things might have been if you hadn't done any magic, and taking that as imagined evidence of its impact, then it should be a red flag. Even if such generous assessments were true, these easy narratives signal that your ability to reasonably assess whether your magic is actually doing anything has become compromised. There is comfort to be had in making yourself feel as if you have done something in situations where you would otherwise be powerless, and even that can be a catalyst for reclaiming lost agency and changing a self-defeating pattern. But if your starting premise had been to do more than instigate an internal process, then it is insincere to move the goalposts after the fact when more tangible results are not forthcoming.

Worse, there are pitfalls to avoid in replacing any definitive action towards change with only the feeling of having taken an action. Don't let your magic be only a soothing balm for a bruised ego. Keep it real, and as much as possible, keep it trained on finite and unambiguous outcomes that give you greater capacity to gauge what is and is not happening. Without that, there is no basis for adjusting, modifying, working an alternative angle, or changing approach in response to a shifting scenario. There is no basis for studying the interplay of your sorcerous strategy and a live situation, and it is the cultivation of that responsive dexterity that makes for tasty sorcery.

There's skill to be had in this work apart from just knowing how to accomplish the practical dynamics of sorcerous acts. Magicians can overlook that and place their focus on obtaining ever more elaborate ceremonial moves or heightened states or ever rarer ingredients, while deploying it all sloppily. The artfulness of operative magic is not so much in knowing how to hit, but understanding where to hit and when, and to what end.

While we can establish as a premise that one's likely reach may be limited without personal concerns of the target, and ideally some manner of legit initiation or sorcerous pacts behind you – it is also true that even a stray evil eye from an uncultivated natural witch might pose problems for a target if it happens to land in the worst possible place and at the worst possible time, upsetting an already delicate or precarious existing predicament in the target's life.

Public life and the personalities drawn to the political sphere are often stacked with precarious predicaments that may be susceptible to the hand of the upsetter. Aim directly at the big figurehead targets and your enflamed intent is instantly awash amid the dreaming of a nation if not a world. A drop in an ocean of competing wishes and tempestuous hopes.

UPSETTER

Magicians are sneaky bastards, at least in all the stories. They will step to you with sleight and misdirection, not the headlong charge. The nature of their danger is not the forceful flail, it's the thing that you were never expecting. The unfortunate coincidence or outside chance that catches you off guard, or the slow rot that set into all the places where you were not looking.

The magic you should be afraid of is not going to come from the posturing assailant telegraphing every move, sometimes literally on social media. It's the battles that have already been waged and won before you notice them. The knife that sticks you while your attention is elsewhere. The wickedness worked upon your weak points and blind spots.

Conjuration that targets existing tendencies in your personality and simply feeds and exacerbates these qualities so that you tear your own life apart. Sorcery that can take a snapshot of the patterns and processes moving through a target's unfolding situation – by geomantic chart or spread of cards – and discern precisely which influences to dampen or enflame. The opposite of what you would look for in a reading thrown to stabilize and empower a client. Magic that knows about a small fire before you do, and pours petrol on it while dampening your capacity for noticing it or your ability to put it out.

Such methods of inquiry may also be used to take the temperature of harder targets, which may be resistant to a direct upset, but could perhaps be undermined or have their foundation chipped away at in such a way that destabilizes and encourages entropy and collapse. Political structure X may appear unshakeable to confront head-on, but how much of its stability is dependent on uneasy alliance and fragile coalition of divergent interest. Candidate Y might look like they have it all sewn up, but how much of their slickness and agility is supported by the hard work of other individuals in their campaign, and what fissures can be exploited within the organizational structure that their effectiveness relies upon?

Ideologies that condone or revel in unambiguous cruelty to groups perceived as undesirable are often populated by operators who are themselves damaged or insecure in some way. Fascism imagines itself a bundle of sticks bound together for strength, but at the operational level, you're more likely to find a shark tank seething with petty resentment and barely repressed rivalry. Subtle sorcery won't try to butt its head against the outside bark of the bundle, when it can scry for specks of rot within and cultivate epidemic conditions for the blight to aggressively take hold. A culture that lauds and rewards boisterous displays of machismo can have its own imagined strength turned back upon itself as a weapon. The misplaced confidence that is heated into disastrous overconfidence, the daring power play that backfires and ends in ruin.

Sorcery travels along vectors of potentiality and when it comes to fruition it will often be embedded in the flux of life as if its unfolding were inevitable, even if the chances of its manifestation may have appeared precarious or unlikely before the work was done. Work can be crafted with subtlety so that the recipient never has any reason to suspect anything has been put down upon them. As the target of such work, it can feel as if you made it all come apart on your own, except you didn't.

Looking after a patch is the tried and true dynamic for operative sorcery. A magic concerned with causing real world change to occur in the here and now, must by necessity orient itself in the here and now with material ingredients, physical links, connection to place and the spirits of place. Ground it somewhere, if you want your work to take root and flourish in the garden of the present.

Consider how any distant, harder targets that sit outside your immediate sphere of influence may have levers closer to home. Peer into the political ecosystem that you hope to impact and look for a loose thread within your grasp that might invite further unraveling. Do your part locally, taking care of imbalances and injustices within your immediate sphere, according to your own nature and calling. But have an eye on the bigger picture, and the way that small correctives can add up and shape an underlying landscape or sway neutral decisions in a preferred direction. Ascertain the dominos that might be toppled from your seat at the table and create auguries for the path of their trajectory and what they might set in motion.

It doesn't need to be complicated, but it does need to be tidy. Identify what you're going to support and then support it with sustained work on its behalf. Fix a crown of success above the head of a candidate for office. Set them in a jar with bay leaves and basil. Allspice, orange peel, cinnamon and cloves. Strong roots. Sugar for sweetness. Calamus for influence. Deer's tongue for eloquence. Protection from enemies. Work to open roads and break down obstacles. Psalms 47 and 65. Talismans of the Sun and Jupiter. Participate in the specifics of a campaign with this work and begin as early as possible. Adapt to changing circumstance.

Souring and slowing works may be done to quell and disempower opponents. It can be on people but it doesn't need to be. Campaigns and think tanks and similar institutions can be worked upon with some of the same formulary and moves as court case work. Inflammatory confusion powders strewn around outside an office. Candles burned to stupefy. Work to block roads or cloud minds. Adaptations of hot foot that make an organization too heated and uncomfortable for employees to want to stay there for any length of time. Crossing up a company's financial luck and feeding its will to fail. Tapa boca hour for petty demagogues and youtube propagandists.

Campaign logo and photos of key players inside of a lemon cut in half and stuck back together with pins. Sunken into a jar with dirt gathered and paid for from the four corners of a campaign office or similar. Black mustard seed. Poppy seed. Red pepper. Souring vinegar. Psalms 43 and 55. Jar turned upside down and a black candle burned on the regular to work the condition. Learn how to add nuance to each work that better customizes its parameters to the specifics of the situation at hand. Don't tie knots that you will regret.

Watch your back. Tighten up the protection. Have precautions in place that no-one knows about. Place as much emphasis on these efforts as you give to any politically oriented sorcery. Prepare for potential consequence and kickback, and close up as many trackways of trouble as you can conceive of and remedy.

Don't show your hand. Learn work to hide the work. Surround yourself with tricks and traps and obfuscation. Never make it easy for anyone who comes to call with malicious intent.

Build a repertoire of spiritual baths for diverse purpose. Simple and regular is better than complicated and infrequent. Wash down your doors, windows and floors. Clean the grime. Make uncrossing and reversing moves a part of your routine. Don't charge into anything without sufficient preparation and clean up after yourself following any hot or heavy gear with thorough cleansing and holy works.

High net worth and ultra-high net worth power brokers will not hesitate for an instant to wield their influence in accordance with their personal ideology or to further their own interests. Magic might then be seen as a counter-balance, and more than that, if it hears the tune of the dead and the whisper of the land. Here comes a candle to light you to bed, here comes a chopper to chop off your head. The sea is coming. Broken futures crowd the second sight. Clogged crystal ball and soggy tea leaves.

Active sorcery can make a difference, but the personal is also political. Bottles of influence and powders of bewilderment are secondary to the everyday footfall of attrition posed by the steady drip of living magic. Insistent, resilient memory that endures beyond the long cons and predatory hucksters. Soil of the dead and cacophony of branches. Undaunted in its purpose, staunch against proselytism and distortion, constant in the spell it casts. Change is woven in the smallest of everyday choices. The micro-decisions that you make moment to moment, and which determine what your magic is about. What you will stand for, and what you will not. What you choose to cultivate and nourish within your orbit, and what you will close the door upon and send on its way. The final shape of the spell that you are casting from cradle to grave. Magic that can hear the imperative of the dead and the wild murmur of the land, and will act from this foundational point, tending its patch and taking the knife to weeds that strangle. Magic that has an ear for rebellious roadside spirit and inner city undine, churchyard ghost and blood ancestor. Magic that will not break or bend to the latest deceiver or be captivated by their bag of tricks. Magic that will not sit at your table. Magic that will never obey you. Magic that you will never defeat. You can crush us, you can bruise us, but you have to answer to –

REVIEWS

SECRETS OF SOLOMON:
A Witch's Handbook from the trial records of the Venetian Inquisition

Edited and translated by Joseph H. Peterson

Reviewed by Jake Stratton-Kent

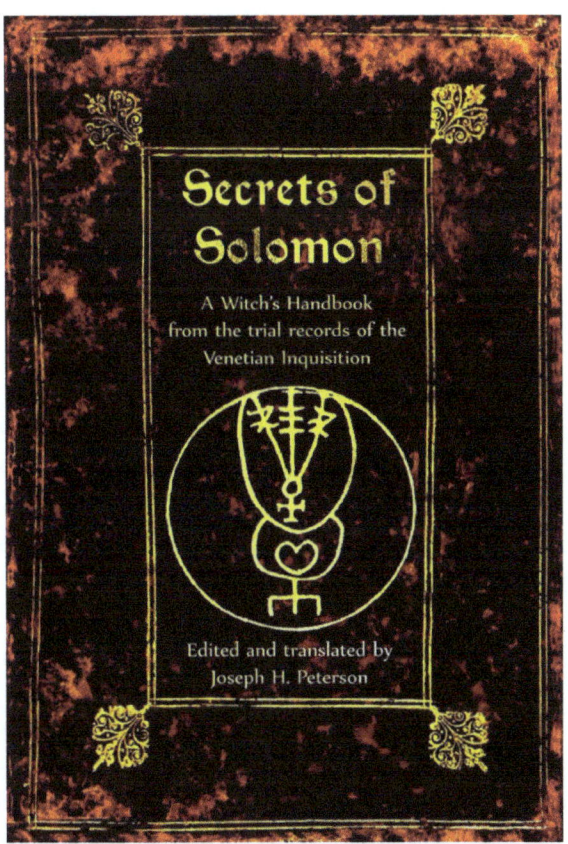

"This grimoire, or handbook of magic, was confiscated by the Venetian Inquisition in 1636 from practicing witches. After decades of searching for this elusive text, I now have the pleasure of presenting and translating it here for the first time. It contains their secret techniques for dealing with the more dangerous spirits or daemons, intentionally scattered and hidden within a collection of "secrets" comprising many detailed examples. Together these provide enough clues to enable practitioners to create their own spells for working with all the spirits cataloged. It distinguishes itself as a supplement to the better known Clavicula Salomonis ("Key of Solomon"); whereas that text focuses on aerial spirits, this one focuses on chthonic spirits. This text is one of the primary original sources for the popular Grimorium Verum."

This is an important addition to *Grimorium Verum* studies, a subject that increasingly requires a section of its own on informed bookshelves. A section with more than one of Joseph's titles thereon, and, as he has been kind enough to mention, one or two of mine. As readers of his previous editions of the grimoires would expect, the critical apparatus is superbly executed and a model of clarity.

An erudite subject for future chronicler exegetes is the order of publication by various authors during the current grimoire explosion, and how the overlaps and intervals resolve. Relevant here is that JHP/JSK's GVs were virtually simultaneous and cordially independent. Skinner & Rankine's *Veritable Keys* though earlier was not consulted for TG, my access to the GV's 'predecessor MSS' (sic) was through Joseph's excellent website. Likewise, Joseph's *Oberon* and my *Pandemonium* also overlapped, in content and time but without collusion, and came to identical conclusions regarding certain spirit hierarchies and numerous individual spirits within them. My conclusions in the latter volume regarding the original identity of Scirlin and Syrach (and, subsequently, Lucifuge Rofocale) are not incorporated in *Secrets* but make practical sense as well as having support via 'literary exegesis'.

It is the first of the four books in the *Secrets of Solomon*, which deals with the 'chthonic' spirits, that has most in common with the GV; it is also where I am best qualified as a reviewer. The catalogue of spirits is clearly all but identical to the 'First Part' of the GV. However, GVs 'Second Part' consists of a series of 'Supernatural Secrets', and states that they all work through the spirits of the First Part. Clearly, while some of them do, others would require very hands on adaptation to do so. In *Secrets* this is not the case, the account of the hierarchy is accompanied directly by operations involving them. The text is very specific that the matter of the pact is cryptically concealed within these details, and 'hands on adaptation' can then extend the formula to any amount of similar operations once it is grasped. This suggests more editorial comprehension and practical continuity between the *Secrets* and the GV's 'Supernatural Secrets' than may appear. The *Secrets of Solomon* form involves sophisticated sigil magic and use of magical materia, such as stones and plants. Some of the 'Supernatural Secrets' similarly employ the spirit sigils – all are meant to when adapted as intended in my view – but the use of magical materia has substantially diminished and most of the spells are utterly different. On the other hand, knowledge of the spirit hierarchy as employed in the sigil magic side of *Secrets* is directly employed in the *Third Part* of the GV. That is, working through the chain of command with sigils of superiors, deputies and 'subordinates' is integral to the spells of *Secrets* and the conjurations of the GV. So too, as examination of both will show, the spirit Frimost is emphasised considerably in both approaches &c.

As an operative reader of this literature the 'materia magica' element omitted in the GV (and generally underplayed in 'logocentric' grimoires) has been explored and added to my spell work and emphasised in my writings for some time, as has said 'hands on adaptation'. In the present it is important to recognise that it is native to the tradition and from thence explore for ourselves. It is also important to note that the differences between texts makes neither wrong. The GV – particularly the Alibeck edition – is a continuation and a reworking of the tradition *Secrets* embodies, by a gifted but anonymous practitioner. His, or possibly her, incorporation of Solomonic apparatus and a conjuration process to accompany the spirit hierarchy of the older text is clearly that of an able and informed magician. The diminution of materia magica is to be regretted, but is easily corrected, while his genius in applied sigil magic clearly draws from the same well.

In closing, Joseph is of course absolutely correct to emphasise that this is one of the primary original sources for the GV. That the grimoire's account of the spirit hierarchy could not be derived directly from the Lansdowne 1202 and Wellcome MSS 983 is a matter addressed in *Pandemonium*. In short, its account is superior and supplies omissions in both; this superiority is checkable by various means, some more abstruse than others, but given further support by Joseph's *Secrets*. The matter does not end here, these MSS' account of working with these spirits and 'secrets', while not direct sources for the GV, nevertheless clearly derive from *Secrets*. *Secrets* mentions employing a wand without giving specifics, alluding instead to another work. Yet the MSS mentioned do describe a wand. More significantly, they pair it with a stone, apparently reducing the magician's entire apparatus to these two items. This feature is shared with the *Grand Grimoire*, which is clearly related to the same family of texts and its *modus operandi*. Indeed, once the identity of Syrach and Lucifuge Rofocale is grasped, its account of the deputies is a better match for the older form in its complete state than is the GV.

Other indicators that mysteries remain in the wake of this landmark publication are:

- The appearance of GV forms of the spirit names in the *Grimoire of Pope Honorius*, rather than the differing (and occasionally bizarre) spellings employed in *Secrets*, Wellcome and Lansdowne. I am very much with Joseph that the GV strand is an influence on Honorius rather than vice versa (though later reciprocation did occur). Its preference for the *Verum* forms of the names is both curious and suggestive, but hard to date precisely.
- The appearance of GV forms of the sigils – particularly that of Silcharde – on the pact of Urban Grandier (trial records 1629-1634), which is just prior to *Secrets* itself (Inquisition records 1636).

In closing this incomplete review – there are three further treatises in *Secrets* – I congratulate Joseph on this most excellent publication. Considering his expenditure in time and labour following the papertrail, the very low price of the paperback edition further commends him and his work. This is a book not to be missed by earnest students of the grimoires.

AUTHORS

JACK GRAYLE is the author of THE HEKATAEON, a grimoire published by IXAXAAR in 2019. He has led devotional rites to Hekate at Black Flame PDX and the Left Hand Path Consortium, and he currently teaches online classes on Hekatean sorcery for The Blackthorne School. He has performed Shakespeare in London and New York City, and is a Grammy-nominated audiobook narrator.

CATH THOMPSON is an English Qaballist and Stellar Magickian of nearly 40 years experience. In 1980 she became the youngest initiated member of James Lees' O∴A∴A∴ and she is the archivist of the group's many layered occult invesigations. These included the application of astrological principles to ceremonial magick, and the pioneering research and development of the English Qaballa, which Lees discovered in 1976 – groundbreaking work that continues to this day, and to which she has contributed in no small measure.

MANI C. PRICE is a NYC visionary artist who paints ordinary women into exotic, self-empowered goddesses. Her work focuses on exploring women's sexual empowerment, and the idea of the divine feminine. Born on the edge of the urban jungle, Mani's work, from paintings to animated films and shorts, has been featured internationally in various galleries, shows, events, e-zines, festivals, and more.

HUMBERTO MAGGI has dug deeply into the textbooks of magic and into the layers of his own psyche, showing throughout his published work a profound grasp of both the esoteric literature of magic and the subtle nature of our relationship to the spirits. In his work we find the struggle between the trained scientific mind and the magician's yearning for supernatural, daemonic experience, the ecstatic awakening which is the key feature of Maggi's endeavours.

GAVIN FOX is a freelance occult author currently residing in the UK. He specialises in creating engaging and informative longform articles on a variety of weird and unusual topics. These include chaos magick, necromancy, paranormal investigation and the unfair treatment of his fellow occultists both past and present. He maintains a portfolio of his previous published work at thevulpineportfolio.com and can be contacted through his social media presence at facebook.com/TheVulpinePortfolio.

ELDRED HIERONYMUS WORMWOOD is a folklorist, antiquarian, folkwitch and book collector living in London. He is the editor of the *Skeptical Occultist*, the *Folkwitch* journal, and the proprietor of Alkahest Press. His research into the folklore of Morocco and Portugal, in particular the apotropaic markings of rural agricultural buildings, is ongoing. When not haunting the shelves of various bookshops and private libraries he can be found digging among ruins for clues to mankind's forgotten past. Follow his adventures at skepticaloccultist.com.

J SWOFFORD is an artist living and working in beautiful Portland, Oregon, USA. The son of creative parents, he was given the letter J as his first full name at birth. He is fascinated by the mysteries of mythology and folklore and uses art and photography to explore things seen and unseen. He holds a BFA in Photography from the Oregon College of Art & Craft. He has exhibited his artwork across the United States and internationally.

ERICA FREVEL is an esoteric artist and devotee of the Void. Her lifelong mystical devotional practice has led to extensive occult and academic research. Experimentation in dream yoga, automatic writing, black magick and demonic channeling techniques are applied to a fine art praxis in her combination ritual chamber/art studio/occult library. She writes independently and within her secret society of devotees.

Verónica Rivas (Melong Yeshe) is an Uruguayan author and researcher based in Brazil. Her cosmological and anthropological studies in magical practices among Eastern cultures led her to become interested in healing techniques. When she became a Reiki Master, she started to research the possibilities of integrating Reiki techniques with other ways of working with Energy, using her academic training in Philosophy as an epistemological background. She is also an initiated and practitioner of Vajrayana Buddhism (Esoteric Buddhism) focusing her practical work on the deity known as Kurukulla. Currently her research is focused on female deities and spirits of the Vajrayana and Hindu traditions and Maria de Padilla and her connection with Quimbanda.

Victoria Musson is a natural fibre artist who follows the seasons of the agricultural year, celebrating them through traditional folk magic and cunning craft. Her homeland is the gentle undulating South Derbyshire landscape where she enjoys the hidden sacred country and the folklore and magic of the land. She has walked upon these soils all her life and witnessed first hand the joys and sorrows that nature controls. We are surrounded by magic and usually walk straight past it as our modern eyes are closed to the subtle ways it reveals itself. The Devil they say is in the detail, and so he is.

Anthony Nine is a writer and artist from the UK, now based in Miami. His work explores intersecting themes of occultism, African Diaspora traditions, psychogeography, music and culture. He is the author of *Space Weather Report*, a colouring book account of the world of spirit, available from Revelore Press.

ADVERTISEMENTS

GUIDES TO THE UNDERWORLD
Hadean's collection of pamphlets for the discerning reader.
WWW.HADEANPRESS.COM

Midian Books

Occult, counterculture and curious books and ephemera, old and new.
Email lists sent regularly.

www.midianbooks.com

Online mail order shop specialising in Occult Curioddities, Object D'art, Vintage and Rare Tarot and Divination. Also the exclusive retail outlet for the creations of Folk Artist Victoria Musson. Goddesses and idols a speciality.

Online shop

www.mrsmidian.co.uk

Artist website

www.victoriamusson.com

Book hypnotherapy sessions to:
- Boost your magical abilities.
- Get yourself out of the armchair.
- Free yourself from anxiety.
- Free yourself from inner conflict.

Book for a private lesson to learn:
- How to induce hypnosis in others.
- Self hypnosis and parts therapy.
- A unique spirit contact tech.

Contact: mail@lancebaker.net

CROSSROADS SORCERY
OCCULT SERVICES AND SUPPLIES
OILS, INCENSE, SOAPS
RITUAL TOOLS, SCRYING MIRRORS
SPIRITUAL WORK

WWW.CROSSROADSSORCERY.COM

Space Weather Report

A very normal colouring book by Anthony Nine that is definitely not a spell. Nothing like that. Available from Revelore.com.

"Lets the outsideness come sneaking in whilst your back is turned. Words that beguile and befuddle. Black lines of flight given shape flesh out to unhoped-for vistas unfolding under crayon and pencil." – Phil Hine

www.ingramcontent.com/pod-product-compliance
Lightning Source LLC
Chambersburg PA
CBHW041239240426

43668CB00022B/2442